MIND
OVER
RISK

MIND OVER RISK

Leading a Safety Culture Revolution

By Bo Brown

THINKSAFE STRATEGIES LLC
SAFETY IS A MINDSET

The content associated with this book is the sole work and responsibility of the author. Gatekeeper Press had no involvement in the generation of this content.

Mind over Risk: Leading a Safety Culture Revolution

Published by Gatekeeper Press
7853 Gunn Hwy., Suite 209
Tampa, FL 33626
www.GatekeeperPress.com

Copyright © 2024 by Bo Brown
All rights reserved. Neither this book, nor any parts within it may be sold or reproduced in any form or by any electronic or mechanical means, including information storage and retrieval systems, without permission in writing from the author. The only exception is by a reviewer, who may quote short excerpts in a review.

The editorial work for this book are entirely the product of the author. Gatekeeper Press did not participate in and is not responsible for any aspect of these elements.

Library of Congress Control Number:

ISBN (paperback): 9781662957840
eISBN: 9781662957970

Table of Contents

Introduction		vii
Chapter 1	Understanding the Importance of a Safety Mindset	1
Chapter 2	Personal Accountability: Owning Safety	9
Chapter 3	Adopting a Questioning Attitude	21
Chapter 4	Leadership: Guiding the Safety Culture	30
Chapter 5	Modeling the Behavior You Seek	42
Chapter 6	The Power of Mentoring in Building a Safety-First Culture	53
Chapter 7	Building Strong Relationships for a Safer Workplace	64
Chapter 8	Implementing Safety Tools and Checklists for Consistency and Accountability	76
Chapter 9	Real-Life Experiences and Lessons Learned	93
Chapter 10	Sustaining a Safety Culture for the Future	104
References		116
About the Author		119

Introduction

Safety is more than just following a set of rules—it is a mindset, a culture, and a personal responsibility that affects every level of an organization. Safety must become a core value in the electrical utility industry, where workers face complex and high-risk environments daily. Every worker must internalize safety principles, from the newest apprentice to the most experienced foreman. It is about more than just compliance—cultivating a **safety-first mindset** where individuals take ownership of their well-being and those around them.

The margin for error is incredibly small in industries like this one, where electrical hazards, elevated workspaces, heavy equipment, and unpredictable environmental conditions are part of everyday operations. A single misstep can result in severe injury, fatalities, and long-lasting consequences for the entire crew. Yet, the difference between a near miss and a tragedy often comes down to the decisions made at the moment. This is why developing a safety mindset, a questioning attitude, and personal accountability are vital to sustaining a safety culture that eliminates preventable accidents.

The Need for a Shift in Safety Culture

This book, *Mind over Risk: Leading a Safety Culture Revolution,* is not just a guide on safety procedures—it's a framework for shifting the way safety is approached, understood, and implemented in the workplace. It is designed to create a lasting impact on how individuals and organizations view safety. We are moving beyond the traditional model where safety is someone else's job or just a checklist to complete before a task. Instead, the goal is to make **every worker a guardian of safety**, constantly vigilant and responsible for protecting themselves and their team.

Safety culture is about more than regulatory compliance or passing audits—it's about embedding safety into the organization's very fabric. This involves developing a mindset where safety is not a chore but an instinct, where every task, decision, and action is filtered through the lens of safety.

A shift in safety culture begins with the understanding that **safety isn't static**. It's an evolving process requiring continuous learning, engagement, and leadership. Safety cannot be achieved with a single training session or policy—it's a commitment that must be renewed daily, with each person playing their part in making the workplace safer.

Introduction

The Core of a Safety Mindset: Proactivity, Accountability, and Relationships

This book is structured around three essential pillars that form the foundation of a sustainable safety culture:

1. **Proactivity:** The most effective way to prevent accidents is to **anticipate risks** before they become problems. Workers must adopt a questioning attitude—constantly asking themselves and their peers: *What could go wrong? What are the hazards in this task? Have we taken every precaution?* Instead of reacting to incidents, a proactive approach identifies hazards early and mitigates them before they lead to accidents.
2. **Personal Accountability:** Safety is everyone's responsibility, and the first step in creating a safety-first mindset is **taking ownership** of your actions. This includes following procedures, wearing appropriate PPE, and being vigilant. But it also means going beyond compliance—being accountable for yourself and your team. Personal accountability is a key factor in preventing incidents and includes owning up to mistakes and near misses, using them as learning opportunities, and continually striving to improve.
3. **Building Strong Relationships:** Safety is not a solitary effort—it's a **team commitment**. Building

strong, trusting relationships between workers, supervisors, and leadership creates a safety net beyond personal actions. When team members trust each other, they are more likely to speak up, share concerns, and watch for each other's safety. A successful safety culture is rooted in strong interpersonal connections and open communication, where everyone's voice is valued and empowered to call out unsafe conditions without fear of retaliation. A shared responsibility and a sense of unity binds us all in our commitment to safety.

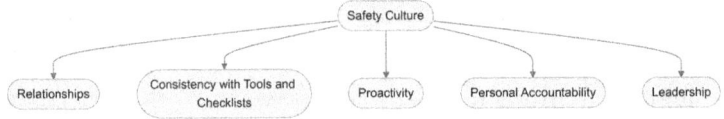

What This Book Offers

This book aims to provide a roadmap for transforming safety culture in the electrical utility industry through strategies, real-life examples, and actionable tools. You'll learn about:

- **The Power of Leadership in Safety:** Leaders set the tone for safety in the workplace. Their actions, attitudes, and priorities influence how workers perceive and approach safety. In this book, you'll explore how leadership can model safety behaviors, establish clear expectations, and foster an environment where safety is always the top priority. Leadership's influence in promoting a safety culture cannot be overstated.

- **Mentorship and Its Role in Cultivating a Safety-First Culture:** Mentorship is an invaluable tool in shaping the safety behaviors of less experienced workers. By pairing seasoned workers with new hires, organizations can ensure that the next generation of workers internalizes safety as a core value from day one. You'll discover how your effective mentorship transfers technical skills and fosters a deep commitment to safety through hands-on guidance and relationship-building, making you a crucial part of the safety culture transformation.
- **Practical Tools and Checklists to Drive Consistency:** Safety isn't just a mindset—it requires structure. The book provides visualized checklists, task-specific safety protocols, and practical tools that can be integrated into daily workflows. These tools help eliminate human error, standardize safety practices, and ensure that every worker has a clear, actionable path to following safety procedures.
- **Real-Life Experiences and Lessons Learned:** Sometimes, the best lessons come from real-world incidents. Through case studies of accidents, near misses, and safety successes, this book offers

insight into what went wrong, how it could have been prevented, and what changes were implemented afterward. These stories emphasize that **safety is a continuous journey**, not a destination, and learning from past experiences is key to preventing future incidents. By understanding these experiences, we can better prepare for the challenges ahead.
- **Sustaining a Safety Culture for the Future:** Safety culture is not a one-time initiative—it must evolve and be sustained as the organization grows. The final chapter focuses on how organizations can ensure their safety culture remains strong, even as new technologies, processes, and challenges emerge. It emphasizes the importance of **continuous improvement, leadership involvement, and innovation** to keep safety at the forefront of every decision. Safety culture is not a destination but a continuous journey that requires ongoing commitment and vigilance.

The Goal: A Safer Tomorrow

The ultimate goal of this book is simple but profound: to ensure that every worker goes home safe at the end of the day. We can prevent accidents and protect lives by adopting a safety-first mindset, cultivating personal accountability, and building a proactive, supportive safety culture.

Introduction

By reading this book, you are taking an important step toward transforming how you, your team, and your organization view and approach safety. Whether you're a seasoned line worker, a team leader, or a company executive, the insights and tools in this book will help you strengthen your safety culture, reduce incidents, and ensure that safety becomes an instinctive part of your day-to-day operations.

Remember, safety is not just about compliance—it's about caring for yourself, your team, and your community. When safety becomes part of your mindset, the ripple effect spreads throughout the organization, creating an environment where everyone looks out for one another.

Welcome to the journey of building and sustaining a safety-first culture.

Chapter 1

Understanding the Importance of a Safety Mindset

Introduction

In the electrical utility industry, every action carries significant risk, no matter how small. High voltage, working at heights, and exposure to environmental hazards make this one of the most dangerous industries globally. Developing and sustaining a safety mindset is not just about following rules—it's about embedding safety into every decision and action, understanding its importance, and accepting responsibility for one's own safety and the safety of others.

This chapter will introduce you to the core concepts of a safety mindset, why it's vital in our industry, and how you can cultivate it as an individual and a team.

The Impact of Safety Incidents

Before we can fully understand the importance of a safety mindset, it's critical to recognize the impact of safety incidents. When an accident occurs in the electrical utility industry, the consequences are often severe. These incidents can lead to:

- Serious Injuries or Death: Even a minor mistake can be fatal in high voltage and hazardous environments. Falls, electrical burns, electrocutions, and equipment-related injuries are common and often irreversible.
- Psychological Impact on Teams: When a team member is injured, it affects everyone. Colleagues may feel guilt, fear, or anxiety, which can impair their focus and ability to work safely in the future.
- Financial and Legal Repercussions: Accidents can result in hefty fines, increased insurance premiums, and potential legal action. These costs can cripple smaller contractors and erode the profitability of larger utilities.
- Reputation Damage: Companies with poor safety records struggle to attract and retain top talent, and clients may look elsewhere for safer alternatives.

Example: Consider a scenario where a lineman bypasses safety protocols to speed up a job. Unaware of the hazard, a coworker comes into contact with an energized line. The incident could result in severe injury or even death, affecting not only the worker but also the crew, their families, and the company's reputation. The simple act of following safety procedures could have prevented the accident.

Defining a Safety Mindset

A safety mindset is a mental framework prioritizing safety above all other concerns. It's not just about avoiding accidents; it's about being constantly aware of potential hazards and actively seeking to mitigate them. It involves:

- Proactive Thinking: Anticipating risks before they become problems.
- Consistent Vigilance: Always be aware of your surroundings and potential hazards.
- Commitment to Best Practices: Adhering to established safety protocols, even under pressure or time constraints.

Having a safety mindset means understanding that shortcuts may save time temporarily but can have catastrophic consequences. It's about realizing that the cost of safety lapses is far greater than the effort needed to work safely.

The Unique Risks in the Electrical Utility Industry

The electrical utility industry presents specific risks that make cultivating a safety mindset even more critical. These include:

- High-Voltage Equipment: Electrical current is invisible, making it a silent but deadly risk. Even experienced workers can become complacent and fall victim.
- Working at Heights: Falls are a significant cause of injury and death. A lapse in attention or failure to wear fall protection can be fatal.
- Weather Conditions: Powerline work often occurs outdoors, exposing workers to extreme weather, which can make tasks more hazardous.
- Complex and Dynamic Environments: Job sites vary, and each presents different challenges, from equipment hazards to traffic risks.

Example: In a real-life case, a utility worker was electrocuted while working in a confined space. Investigation revealed that poor communication and failure to follow the lockout/tagout procedure were the primary causes. These errors, born from a rushed job, underscore the need for a strong safety mindset and adherence to protocols.

How Mindset Influences Behavior and Outcomes

Your mindset directly influences your behavior. If you have a safety-first mindset, your actions will naturally follow that approach. Conversely, accidents

Understanding the Importance of a Safety Mindset

become inevitable if your mindset prioritizes speed or efficiency at the cost of safety. Here's how mindset affects outcomes:

- **Awareness and Attention:** A safety-focused mindset encourages constant attention to detail. Workers are more likely to spot potential hazards and take the necessary steps to mitigate them.
- **Decision-Making:** Workers with a safety mindset make decisions that prioritize long-term well-being over short-term gains. For example, they will take the time to inspect equipment, wear the appropriate PPE, and ensure that they and their colleagues follow safety protocols, even if it means missing a deadline.
- **Peer Influence:** When individuals adopt a safety mindset, it spreads through the team. Colleagues are more likely to hold each other accountable, and safety practices become part of the group's culture.

Real-Life Experience: A foreman at a utility company I worked with shared a story of a crew member who always ensured that safety briefings were thorough. His diligence and proactive attitude saved the crew from multiple potential incidents. His safety-first mindset became a benchmark for others, and soon, the entire team adopted his approach.

Developing a Safety Mindset

Now that we understand the importance of a safety mindset, how can you develop and reinforce it in your daily work? Here are a few strategies:

1. **Education and Training:** Regularly participate in safety training and update your knowledge of safety protocols. Stay informed about the latest best practices and industry standards.
2. **Reflect on Past Incidents:** Learn from past accidents or near misses. Reflect on what went wrong and how it could have been avoided. Share these lessons with your team to prevent similar incidents.
3. **Engage in Safety Discussions:** Encourage open communication about safety. Share your concerns, ideas, and observations with supervisors and colleagues.
4. **Stay Vigilant, Even During Routine Tasks:** Complacency often sets in during repetitive tasks. Commit to approaching every task with the same level of care and attention, regardless of how routine it may seem.
5. **Personal Accountability:** Understand that safety begins with you. While leadership and systems are critical, personal accountability ensures you contribute to the safety culture rather than undermine it.

Tips for Cultivating a Safety-First Mindset

Here are some actionable tips to help develop and maintain a safety mindset:

- **Perform Pre-Job Safety Briefings**: Always conduct and participate in a pre-job briefing. Identify hazards, review the work plan, and ensure everyone understands their role in maintaining safety.
- **Embrace Continuous Learning:** Safety standards evolve, and so should your knowledge. Attending training sessions, reading safety bulletins, and stay informed about industry trends.
- **Speak Up:** Never be afraid to question a task or procedure if you believe there's a safety risk. It's better to stop work and reassess than to proceed and face a potential accident.
- **Lead by Example:** Whether you're in a formal leadership position or not, model the safety behaviors you expect from others. This includes always wearing PPE, following procedures, and maintaining a questioning attitude.
- **Evaluate Your Own Actions Daily:** At the end of every workday, ask yourself: "Did I do everything I could to work safely today?" Self-reflection can be a powerful tool for maintaining accountability.

Conclusion

A safety mindset is not a one-time achievement but a continuous commitment to vigilance, education, and personal accountability. In the electrical industry, where the stakes are high, cultivating and maintaining this mindset is the difference between a safe, productive career and life-altering accidents. As you move forward in your role, remember that safety starts with you—and it's your responsibility to prioritize it every day.

Chapter 2

Personal Accountability: Owning Safety

Introduction

Safety is not just the responsibility of supervisors or safety officers—it's the personal responsibility of every individual on the job site. In the electrical utility industry, where the risks are high, and the consequences of mistakes can be life-altering, each worker must take ownership of their actions and decisions. **Personal accountability** means understanding that safety begins with you and recognizing that your choices can impact your safety and everyone around you.

This chapter will explore the concept of personal accountability in the context of workplace safety. It will discuss why owning safety is crucial, provide practical steps for fostering personal responsibility, and illustrate how a culture of accountability can significantly reduce incidents and injuries.

What Is Personal Accountability in Safety?

Personal accountability in safety means that every worker takes ownership of their behavior, actions, and decisions as they relate to creating a safe work environment. It's about recognizing that safety is not someone else's responsibility but yours, and that maintaining a safe worksite requires continuous vigilance, decision-making, and action.

The Mindset of Accountability

The mindset of personal accountability starts with the understanding that **you are the first line of defense** when it comes to safety. While safety supervisors and procedures play a role, every individual must take proactive steps to ensure they are working safely and in accordance with safety protocols.

- **Proactive Approach:** Taking the initiative to identify potential hazards, follow safety protocols, and address unsafe conditions, even if it's not in your direct job description.
- **Responsibility for Actions:** Acknowledging that every decision—from wearing PPE to reporting hazards—has consequences. Personal accountability means not waiting for someone else to intervene when a problem arises.

Ownership Beyond Compliance

It is easy to think of safety as following a set of rules and regulations, but personal accountability goes beyond mere compliance. It involves a deeper commitment to the **why** behind the rules, understanding that these protocols are designed to protect lives—not just to avoid penalties or fines.

- **Engagement in Safety Culture:** Personal accountability involves actively participating in safety discussions, briefings, and initiatives rather than passively following rules. It's about being engaged with the safety culture at every level of the organization.
- **Owning Mistakes:** Accountability also means owning up to mistakes or oversights, reporting near misses, and learning from errors to ensure they are not repeated.

Example: A worker notices that the pre-task briefing skipped a discussion about potential weather hazards. Instead of assuming it's not a big deal, the worker speaks up, ensuring that the team revisits the topic. This accountability act prevents the crew from being caught off-guard by an approaching storm that could have compromised their safety.

The Importance of Personal Accountability in High-Risk Industries

In industries like electrical utility work, the stakes are incredibly high. One mistake can lead to severe injury or death, which makes personal accountability not just important but critical. When workers take responsibility for their actions and decisions, the team benefits from a more cohesive and safety-conscious work environment.

Accountability Reduces Incidents

When workers are accountable for their own safety—and for the safety of others—there is a direct reduction in incidents. Personal accountability leads to:

- **Increased Hazard Awareness:** Workers accountable for their safety are more vigilant in identifying and addressing hazards.
- **Improved Safety Compliance:** Workers who are responsible for their safety are less likely to cut corners, skip safety steps, or take unnecessary risks.
- **Better Communication:** Accountability fosters open communication about safety concerns, leading to faster responses to potential issues.

Example: A lineman took extra time to inspect his harness even though the job was running behind schedule. His decision to prioritize safety prevented a fall when he later discovered a frayed section of his equipment. His accountability in following proper inspection procedures likely saved his life.

Accountability Promotes Peer Safety

Personal accountability isn't just about protecting yourself—it's also about looking out for the safety of your peers. In a safety-conscious culture, workers feel responsible for the safety of everyone around them, not just their own well-being.

- **Peer Accountability:** Workers who take personal responsibility for safety are more likely to intervene if they see a coworker behaving unsafely or making a mistake.
- **Supportive Feedback:** In environments where personal accountability is the norm, workers provide constructive feedback to one another, helping to prevent accidents before they happen.

Example: During a pole replacement, a team member noticed that his colleague wasn't wearing the correct gloves for the task. Rather than ignoring it, he reminded his coworker to switch to insulated gloves, preventing potential electrocution. This culture of accountability ensured that workers looked out for one another's safety.

Fostering a Culture of Accountability

Creating a workplace where personal accountability thrives requires deliberate effort. It's not something that happens overnight, but there are concrete steps that organizations and leaders can take to foster a culture where workers take responsibility for their own safety and the safety of others.

Leading by Example

Accountability starts with leadership. Workers will take their cues from supervisors and managers, which means that leaders must model the behavior they want to see from their teams.

- **Consistent Safety Behavior:** Supervisors must consistently follow safety protocols, demonstrate hazard awareness, and engage in safety discussions to show that they, too, are accountable for safety.
- **Encourage Open Communication:** Leaders should actively encourage workers to voice safety concerns, report near misses, and offer suggestions for improvement. When workers see that their concerns are taken seriously, they are more likely to hold themselves accountable.

Example: A supervisor who insists on full compliance with PPE rules—even during short, seemingly low-risk jobs—sends a message that safety is non-negotiable. Workers are more likely to follow suit when they see their leaders holding themselves accountable.

Establishing Clear Expectations

For personal accountability to thrive, workers need to understand what is expected of them. Organizations should clearly communicate safety expectations, responsibilities, and the importance of taking personal ownership of safety.

- **Define Safety Roles:** Workers should know exactly what is required of them in terms of safety protocols, reporting hazards, and intervening when they see unsafe behavior.
- **Incentivize Accountability:** Recognizing and rewarding workers who demonstrate personal accountability reinforces the idea that safety is a core value. This could involve formal recognition programs, safety bonuses, or public acknowledgment during safety meetings.

Encouraging Self-Reflection

One of the most effective ways to cultivate personal accountability is to encourage workers to reflect on their own behaviors and choices. This reflection can be built into daily routines, safety briefings, or post-job debriefs.

- **Daily Safety Check-Ins:** Encourage workers to ask themselves at the start of each shift, "Am I doing everything I can to work safely today?"
- **Post-Job Reflection:** After each job, workers should reflect on what went well, what could have been done better, and how they can improve their safety practices going forward.

Example: A contracting company implemented a practice where, at the end of each day, every worker wrote down one thing they did to improve safety. This small act of reflection encouraged workers to think about their actions and reinforced the importance of personal accountability in everyday tasks.

Overcoming Barriers to Personal Accountability

Despite its importance, personal accountability can sometimes be difficult to instill. Workers may feel pressured to prioritize speed over safety, or they may be hesitant to speak up when they see unsafe practices. Organizations need to address these barriers to create an environment where accountability can flourish.

Combating Complacency

In any job that involves repetitive tasks, complacency can set in, leading workers to overlook potential hazards or take shortcuts. Overcoming complacency requires constant vigilance and reinforcement of safety protocols.

- **Regular Safety Training:** Continuous education helps workers stay engaged and reminds them of the importance of following safety procedures, even for routine tasks.
- **Rotate Responsibilities:** By rotating job responsibilities, workers are less likely to become complacent, as new tasks keep them alert and engaged.

Example: A lineman who had been with the company for ten years became complacent during a routine line inspection. After almost missing a critical fault in the system, the company introduced rotational duties to keep workers fresh and alert, preventing the kind of mental fatigue that leads to oversights.

Addressing Fear of Speaking Up

In some workplaces, workers may hesitate to speak up about safety concerns, fearing being seen as difficult or confrontational. Organizations must break down this fear to foster personal accountability and encourage a culture of openness.

- **Non-Punitive Reporting:** Workers should be assured that reporting hazards or near misses will never result in punishment but instead be seen as a proactive effort to improve safety.
- **Anonymous Reporting Systems:** Some companies use anonymous reporting tools to encourage workers to share concerns without fear of retaliation, helping to foster a safer, more accountable work environment.

Example: A worker hesitated to report a near miss because he didn't want to be blamed for holding up the job. After introducing an anonymous reporting app, the number of reported near misses increased, helping the company address previously hidden hazards.

Personal Accountability in Action: Real-Life Examples

Personal accountability in safety can be the difference between a near miss and a fatal accident. Here are real-life examples of workers who demonstrated personal accountability and prevented serious incidents.

Example 1: Accountability Prevents a Fall

During a routine line replacement, a worker double-checked his harness despite having already inspected it that morning. He found a small tear in the webbing that had gone unnoticed. By taking the extra step to verify his equipment, he prevented a potential fall from a 40-foot pole.

Lesson: Always double-check your safety gear, even if you've already inspected it. Personal accountability means going the extra mile to ensure your safety.

Example 2: Reporting a Near Miss Saves Lives

A crew member noticed that during a storm restoration, his team was working dangerously close to an energized line that had not been grounded properly. Even though the job was behind schedule, he immediately reported the issue. The crew leader halted the work, and the team corrected the error before any injuries occurred.

Lesson: Don't hesitate to report near misses, even if you think it might slow down the job. Personal accountability means prioritizing safety over speed.

Conclusion

Personal accountability is the foundation of a strong safety culture. In high-risk environments like powerline electrical work, every worker must take ownership of their actions, decisions, and behaviors to ensure not only their own safety but the safety of their team. Organizations can create a safer, more responsible workforce by fostering a mindset of accountability, encouraging open communication, and addressing barriers like complacency and fear of speaking up.

In the next chapter, we'll explore how organizations can continuously improve safety through leadership, innovation, and an unwavering commitment to safety culture.

CHAPTER 3

Adopting a Questioning Attitude

Introduction

A single assumption can lead to dangerous outcomes in the electrical utility industry. Whether you're assuming that a line is de-energized, that your equipment is in perfect working order, or that your team fully understands the task, these unchecked assumptions can escalate into life-threatening situations. Developing a **questioning attitude** is vital to eliminating risks before they become accidents.

A questioning attitude is about being skeptical of the status quo, challenging the assumption that "everything is okay," and actively seeking evidence to confirm safety. In this chapter, we'll discuss the principles behind a questioning attitude, practical ways to apply it on the job, and how it can enhance safety for both individuals and teams.

The Value of a Questioning Attitude

A questioning attitude is the cornerstone of hazard identification and risk mitigation. It's an approach that prevents complacency and fosters a proactive safety culture. By challenging assumptions and looking for gaps in processes, workers are more likely to:

- **Identify Hidden Hazards:** Many dangers in the electrical utility industry are not immediately visible. By asking questions like "Has this equipment been inspected?" or "Are there external factors like weather affecting this job?", workers can uncover potential threats before they cause harm.
- **Avoid Miscommunication:** Misunderstandings between team members are common, and they can be dangerous. A questioning attitude forces everyone to ensure they are on the same page, clarifying instructions and confirming that procedures are understood.
- **Enhance Focus:** Asking questions forces you to stay engaged and mentally alert, which is essential when working in high-risk environments.

Example: In one instance, a worker assumed that a lockout/tagout procedure had been properly followed. Before beginning work, he questioned the assumption, checked the system himself, and found that the equipment was still energized. His questioning attitude likely prevented a serious or even fatal accident.

Principles Behind a Questioning Attitude

Adopting a questioning attitude requires more than simply asking random questions. It involves structured skepticism and a clear understanding of what to look for. Here are some core principles to guide the development of this mindset:

1. **Assume Nothing:** Always assume that something could go wrong unless you've confirmed otherwise. Avoid making assumptions that everything is safe without verification, whether it's a tool's condition or a colleague's readiness.
2. **Seek Evidence:** Don't accept answers without proof. For instance, don't assume a piece of equipment is de-energized unless you have personally tested it with the appropriate tools. Evidence in the form of measurements, inspections, or physical tests is necessary to confirm safety.
3. **Challenge the Routine:** It's easy to become comfortable with routine tasks, but this is where complacency breeds. Even if you've completed a job a hundred times, take the time to review each step and identify potential hazards. Ask yourself, "What could go wrong today?"
4. **Involve the Team:** A questioning attitude isn't just an individual effort. Encourage your team to participate in questioning assumptions and assessing safety. Two sets of eyes are better than one, and

a diverse perspective can help uncover issues that may go unnoticed by a single person.

Real-Life Experience: A crew was tasked with replacing a damaged power pole. The job was routine for the team, but a new crew member questioned whether the pole's height was appropriate for the new voltage being introduced. His questioning led to a review of the specifications, revealing that the original plan was outdated and could have resulted in clearance violations. The simple act of asking a question saved the company from costly rework and ensured compliance with safety standards.

Applying a Questioning Attitude on the Job

Adopting a questioning attitude involves continuously engaging with your work environment and assessing risks at every stage of the job. Here's how to incorporate this attitude into your daily routine:

Pre-Job Briefings

Before starting any task, always ask the following questions:

- What are the known hazards of this job?
- What are the potential hazards that may not be immediately obvious?
- Are all team members aware of their responsibilities and any associated risks?
- What external factors (e.g., weather, nearby activities) could impact safety today?

Pre-job briefings should not be rushed. They are an opportunity to identify, discuss, and address risks before anyone sets foot on the job site.

Visualized Checklist for Pre-Job Briefings

- Have all hazards been identified?
- Have control measures been put in place?
- Have all team members confirmed their understanding of the work scope and safety requirements?

During Work Execution

While the job is underway, the work environment and task dynamics may change. As such, it's important to maintain a questioning attitude throughout the day. Regularly ask:

- Has anything changed that might introduce new hazards?
- Are we following all safety procedures or tempted to take shortcuts?
- Is everyone focused and aware of their surroundings?

A good rule of thumb is to stop and reassess the situation every time you complete a job phase, such as after removing an old line or erecting a new pole. By checking in with yourself and your team, you're more likely to spot developing risks before they escalate.

Post-Job Review

A questioning attitude can help you improve future work after completing the job. Ask:

- Were there any near misses that we didn't anticipate?
- What did we do well, and what could have been better?
- Were there any hazards we missed in the planning stage?

These post-job reviews should be conducted openly and constructively, where all team members are encouraged to share their insights.

Real-Life Case: How a Questioning Attitude Saved a Life

In 2019, a contractor working on a transmission line near a busy highway noticed something unusual—his fall protection gear seemed slightly off, even though it had been inspected earlier in the day. Instead of dismissing his concern, he inspected the gear more closely for a few moments. He discovered a minor tear in the harness that had been overlooked. This questioning attitude led to an immediate gear replacement, potentially saving his life later that day when he was involved in a fall incident. By questioning something that seemed routine, he avoided a serious accident.

Cultivating a Questioning Attitude in Your Team

Encouraging a questioning attitude in the workplace requires a supportive culture where employees feel safe speaking up and challenging assumptions without fear of repercussions. Here's how to foster that environment:

- **Lead by Example:** If you're in a leadership position, demonstrate a questioning attitude in every safety meeting, briefing, and decision. When your team sees you questioning assumptions, they'll feel more comfortable doing the same.

- **Reward Safe Behavior:** Encourage and reward employees who exhibit a questioning attitude. Acknowledge them during team meetings and provide incentives for those who take the extra step to ensure safety.
- **Create a Safe Space for Questions:** Make it clear that no question is too simple or unnecessary when it comes to safety. Ensure that your team knows they can voice concerns at any time without fear of ridicule or reprimand.

Example: A powerline contractor implemented a "question of the day" initiative where each crew member was required to ask a safety-related question during the morning briefing. This initiative helped break down communication barriers and encouraged a culture of vigilance. Over time, the number of safety incidents dropped dramatically as workers became more engaged and thoughtful in their approach.

Tips for Maintaining a Questioning Attitude

To consistently maintain a questioning attitude, here are some practical tips:

1. **Practice Self-Awareness:** Stay alert and continuously scan your environment for hazards. Don't let routine dull your vigilance.

Adopting a Questioning Attitude

2. **Encourage Open Dialogue:** Make questioning a team effort. Encourage your colleagues to voice their concerns and ask questions regularly.
3. **Document Observations:** Keep a safety journal or checklist where you can record any potential risks or areas for improvement that you identify. This helps you stay accountable and also provides valuable insights for future jobs.
4. **Never Be Satisfied with Assumptions:** Even if something seems safe, ask yourself, "What's the worst that could happen?" and act accordingly to prevent it.

Conclusion

Adopting a questioning attitude is essential to preventing accidents in the electrical utility industry. By actively questioning the safety of the work environment, equipment, and procedures, you protect not only yourself but your team. This proactive approach ensures that hidden hazards are identified and addressed before they lead to serious consequences. Remember, it's better to ask a question and delay the job than to move forward with an unsafe assumption.

The next chapter will explore **leadership's role** in guiding and sustaining a strong safety culture—how leaders can inspire and influence a team-wide commitment to safety.

Chapter 4

Leadership: Guiding the Safety Culture

Introduction

In any high-risk industry, such as electrical utility work, leadership plays a crucial role in guiding and sustaining a culture of safety. Effective leaders don't just enforce rules—they inspire their teams to adopt a safety-first mindset. They model the behaviors they expect, mentor their workers, and build relationships rooted in trust and mutual accountability.

This chapter will dive deeper into the specific responsibilities of leadership in shaping safety culture, the different leadership styles that influence safety, and the practical strategies leaders can implement to foster a workplace where safety is not just a priority, but a shared value.

Leadership's Role in Safety

Leaders in the electrical utility industry are responsible for more than ensuring productivity. Their primary duty is to create an environment where workers feel empowered and obligated to prioritize safety. Leaders set the tone for safety in several ways:

- **Establishing Standards and Expectations:** Leaders define what acceptable safety behavior looks like and ensure that everyone understands and follows these expectations.
- **Providing Resources:** Safety isn't possible without the right tools, equipment, and training. Leaders ensure that their teams are properly equipped and that any safety issues are addressed immediately.
- **Creating Accountability:** A good leader holds their team accountable for safety performance, but more importantly, they hold themselves accountable. This means leading by example, consistently following safety protocols, and addressing unsafe behaviors immediately.

Example: A line crew supervisor noticed that his team occasionally bypassed safety harness protocols during quick, low-height pole work. Instead of reprimanding the team without explanation, he gathered the group and demonstrated why even a shortfall could be fatal. He then modeled the proper use of fall protection gear during low-height tasks. The supervisor's proactive, educational approach changed the team's behavior without breeding resentment or fear.

Leadership Styles and Their Influence on Safety

Different leadership styles can have a profound impact on safety culture. While no single style is universally "right" for every situation, understanding how various approaches affect safety is critical for leaders who want to cultivate a strong, safety-conscious workforce. Let's examine a few common leadership styles:

Authoritative Leadership

In authoritative leadership, the leader makes decisions independently, providing clear direction and expectations without much input from the team. This style can be useful in high-risk situations where quick, decisive action is required, especially in emergencies where there's no time for discussion.

However, this approach can also discourage team members from speaking up or challenging unsafe practices if they feel their concerns will be dismissed. In safety, open communication is vital, and authoritative leadership must be balanced with fostering an environment where workers feel safe to raise issues.

Strengths:
- Decisive and clear in high-pressure situations.
- Effective when quick responses are required, such as during emergency repairs.

Weaknesses:
- Can stifle creativity, collaboration, and critical thinking.
- Risks suppressing the questioning attitude necessary for safety.

Participative Leadership

A participative (or democratic) leadership style involves seeking input from team members and making decisions collaboratively. This style encourages communication, trust, and ownership of safety practices. Workers who feel heard and valued are more likely to take responsibility for their own safety and the safety of others.

However, participative leadership can sometimes slow down decision-making, which might be a disadvantage in high-pressure or time-sensitive situations. Leaders must find the right balance between collaboration and decisiveness, particularly when it comes to enforcing safety procedures.

Strengths:
- Fosters a sense of ownership and responsibility for safety.
- Encourages team members to speak up and contribute to improving safety processes.

Weaknesses:
- Can slow down decision-making in urgent scenarios.

- May lead to indecision if too many conflicting opinions arise.

Transformational Leadership

Transformational leaders inspire their teams to go beyond their basic duties, fostering a shared vision of success, including a strong commitment to safety. These leaders are typically charismatic and capable of motivating workers to adopt high-performance standards in safety and productivity.

Transformational leaders are particularly effective at changing organizational culture, instilling safety as a core value, and mentoring team members to take initiative in risk prevention.

Strengths:
- Highly effective at driving cultural change.
- Motivates employees to take personal responsibility for safety.

Weaknesses:
- Requires continuous engagement and charisma to maintain momentum.
- It can be less effective in organizations that are resistant to change.

Servant Leadership

A servant leader prioritizes the needs of their team over their own. They focus on developing their team members and providing them with the resources and support they need to succeed. In the context of safety, this approach can lead to high levels of trust, morale, and engagement, as workers feel cared for and supported.

Servant leadership encourages workers to identify risks and report safety concerns proactively. However, it can also lead to a perceived lack of authority if the leader fails to assert themselves when necessary.

Strengths:
- Build strong relationships and trust.
- Encourages a proactive, engaged approach to safety.

Weaknesses:
- Can be perceived as passive if the leader avoids making difficult decisions.
- Requires balance to ensure authority and accountability are maintained.

Real-Life Example: A transformational leader at a large utility company successfully implemented a new safety initiative. This initiative focused on empowering field teams to lead their own safety briefings, thereby shifting the culture from compliance-driven to ownership-driven safety. The leader's approach led to a significant improvement in safety within six months, with increased near-miss reports indicating a more vigilant workforce and a drop in injury rates.

Practical Leadership Strategies for Safety

Regardless of leadership style, key strategies should be implemented by all safety-focused leaders to foster a strong safety culture. Below are some practical approaches leaders can use to drive safety excellence in the electrical utility industry.

Leading by Example

Leaders must model the behaviors they expect from their team. This includes:

- **Consistently Wearing PPE:** If workers see their supervisor neglecting to wear personal protective equipment (PPE), they may believe cutting corners is acceptable. Ensure that you are always demonstrating proper use of safety gear.
- **Following Safety Protocols:** Take time to perform safety checks, attend briefings, and follow procedures as you expect your team to do.
- **Openly Acknowledge Mistakes**: If you make an error or overlook a safety protocol, admit it openly. This shows your team that everyone is responsible for safety and that mistakes are learning opportunities, not for punishment.

Example: A contracting company supervisor noticed that workers often skipped safety briefings during busy work periods. Instead of reprimanding them, he started arriving early to personally conduct the briefings and emphasized their importance, even on short, routine jobs. Over time, his consistency made the briefings a non-negotiable part of the team's workday.

Mentoring for Safety

Effective safety leadership involves mentoring your team to develop their own safety-first mindset. Mentoring involves:

- **Providing Regular Feedback:** Offer constructive feedback on safety performance in real-time and during formal evaluations.
- **Creating Opportunities for Learning:** Encourage team members to attend safety training and workshops and provide opportunities for them to lead safety initiatives or briefings.

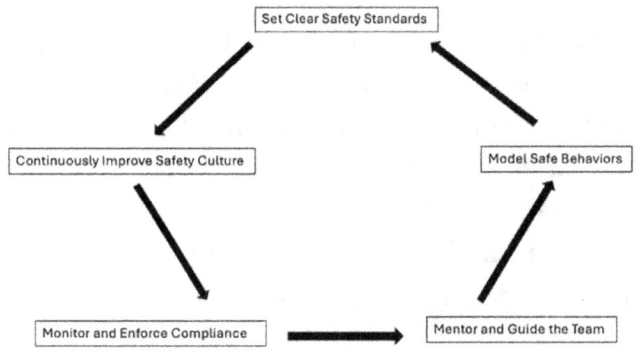

Leadership Safety Process

- **Fostering Accountability:** Every worker should be responsible for not only their own safety but also the safety of their peers. Encourage workers to look out for each other and speak up when they see unsafe behaviors.

Visualized Checklist for Mentoring

1. Have I discussed safety concerns with each team member this week?
2. Have I provided constructive feedback on safety performance recently?
3. Have I encouraged employees to share their own safety insights or lead safety briefings?

Building a Culture of Trust and Communication

Workers need to feel comfortable raising safety concerns without fear of retribution. Leaders must:

- **Encourage Open Communication:** Establish a culture where workers can voice concerns or report hazards. Make it clear that asking safety-related questions is free of consequence.
- **Respond Swiftly to Safety Issues:** Address a safety issue immediately. Even if the concern seems minor, showing that you take safety seriously will encourage workers to keep bringing issues forward.

- **Regular Safety Walkthroughs:** Regularly check job sites to engage with workers and observe potential safety risks firsthand. These walkthroughs should not be treated as audits but as opportunities to listen to the team's concerns.

Example: A manager at a large utility began conducting informal "safety lunches" where workers could openly discuss near-misses and safety challenges without fear of judgment. By fostering open communication in a non-formal setting, the manager built stronger relationships with the team and uncovered several issues that might not have been raised otherwise.

Challenges Leaders Face in Enforcing Safety

While leadership is critical to safety success, it doesn't come without challenges. Common obstacles include:

- **Time Pressure:** In the electrical utility industry, there is often pressured to get jobs done quickly, especially during outages. Leaders must resist the temptation to cut corners on safety in the name of efficiency.
- **Complacency:** Long-time workers or teams who have gone without an incident for extended periods may become complacent. Leaders must actively work to keep safety at the forefront of their minds, even for routine tasks.

- **Resistance to Change:** Some workers may resist new safety protocols, especially if they feel the changes slow them down or add unnecessary complexity. Leaders must effectively communicate the "why" behind the changes and be patient during the adjustment period.

Tips for Effective Safety Leadership

1. **Stay Visible:** As a safety-focused leader, it's important to be present on the job site, observing, listening, and engaging with your team regularly. This visibility builds trust and allows you to address safety issues in real time, demonstrating your commitment to safety and inspiring your team to do the same.
2. **Create a Safety Vision:** Develop a clear vision for what safety looks like in your organization and communicate it often. This vision should be more than just a set of rules; it should be a shared commitment to keeping everyone safe. Ensure everyone on your team understands and buys into this vision, fostering a sense of shared responsibility and commitment to safety.
3. **Encourage Ownership:** Help workers see that safety is not just a top-down responsibility. Encourage them to take ownership of their own safety and to look out for their teammates.

4. **Celebrate Safety Wins:** Celebrate your team's safety milestones, such as achieving zero incidents for a set period. Recognize the hard work and vigilance that went into keeping everyone safe. By celebrating these wins, you acknowledge your team's efforts and reinforce the importance of safety, making everyone feel appreciated and recognized for their contributions to a safe work environment.
5. **Never Compromise on Safety:** No deadline or project is worth risking a life. Always prioritize safety, even if it means missing a deadline or taking longer to complete a job.

Conclusion

Safety leadership is not just about enforcing rules; it's about creating an environment where safety becomes part of the organization's DNA. Leaders must model the behaviors they expect, mentor their teams to take responsibility for safety, and foster a culture of trust, accountability, and open communication. By doing so, leaders can inspire their teams to prioritize safety and a deeply held value.

The next chapter will focus on modeling the behavior you want to see from your team and how that ties into leadership and safety culture.

Chapter 5

Modeling the Behavior You Seek

Introduction

In any industry, especially high-risk ones like powerline electrical work, employees are heavily influenced by the actions and behaviors of their leaders. Regarding safety, nothing speaks louder than what you, as a leader, do daily. Modeling the behavior you seek is one of the most powerful tools at your disposal to shape a strong safety culture. Whether you're a supervisor, manager, or senior crew member, how you approach safety sets the standard for your team.

This chapter will explore how leading by example influences safety culture, the psychological impact of role modeling, and how you can implement practical strategies to model the behaviors you expect from your team. We'll delve into real-world examples, visualized tools, and actionable advice to help you instill safe practices across your workforce.

Why Leading by Example Matters

When leaders visibly follow safety protocols and exhibit a safety-first mindset, it reinforces the importance of those actions for everyone on the team. Workers naturally mirror the behaviors of those in leadership roles, whether consciously or unconsciously. This psychological tendency makes it critical for leaders to be mindful of their own actions, especially in safety-critical environments like electrical utility work.

Here's why modeling behavior matters:

- **Creates Accountability**: When leaders adhere to safety practices, it establishes that no one is exempt from following protocols—everyone is held to the same standard.
- **Builds Trust**: Employees trust leaders who don't just talk about safety but actively demonstrate it. Trust increases team cohesion, making workers more likely to report hazards or offer suggestions for improving safety.
- **Reduces Resistance**: Workers are more likely to comply with safety protocols if they see their supervisors doing the same. On the other hand, if they observe their leaders cutting corners, they'll feel justified in doing so as well.

Example: A crew leader who consistently wears full PPE, even on hot days when it's tempting to skip a layer, sets the tone for the entire crew. His adherence to safety standards, regardless of comfort, demonstrates that safety always comes first. Soon, team members begin to follow suit as they recognize that the standard is non-negotiable.

The Psychology of Role Modeling

It's important to consider how human psychology works to understand the power of modeling behavior, particularly in group settings. People tend to adopt behaviors that are consistent with the actions of those they respect or see as authority figures. In the context of safety, this means that when leaders consistently demonstrate safe practices, workers internalize and imitate those behaviors.

Social Learning Theory

One of the most relevant psychological concepts in leadership is social learning theory, which suggests that people learn behaviors through observation, imitation, and modeling. If employees observe their leaders following safety rules, they are more likely to:

- Internalize those behaviors as norms.
- Feel more obligated to maintain safety standards.
- Hold their peers accountable for safety behaviors as well.
- Mirror neurons and behavior

Neurological studies show that our brains are wired to mimic the behaviors we observe in others. Mirror neurons in our brain fire not only when we perform an action but also when we observe others performing the same action. For example, when a leader checks their harness, dons PPE, or pauses to assess a hazard, workers' brains process those actions as if they were doing them themselves. Over time, these behaviors become ingrained in the team's collective habits.

Real-Life Experience: In one instance, a foreman was consistently seen testing equipment and double-checking lines, even when he wasn't the one working on them. Over time, his crew members began replicating these safety checks, increasing the overall attention to detail on job sites. This subconscious imitation resulted in fewer near-miss incidents.

Practical Ways to Model the Behavior You Want

Modeling the behavior you seek is about more than just following the rules; it's about being intentional and consistent in demonstrating safety-conscious decisions. Below are practical strategies that you can implement to ensure your team follows your lead.

Be Visible on the Job Site

Your presence matters. Workers are more likely to follow safety procedures when they know their leader actively observes and engages with them on-site.

Behavior Impact Cycle

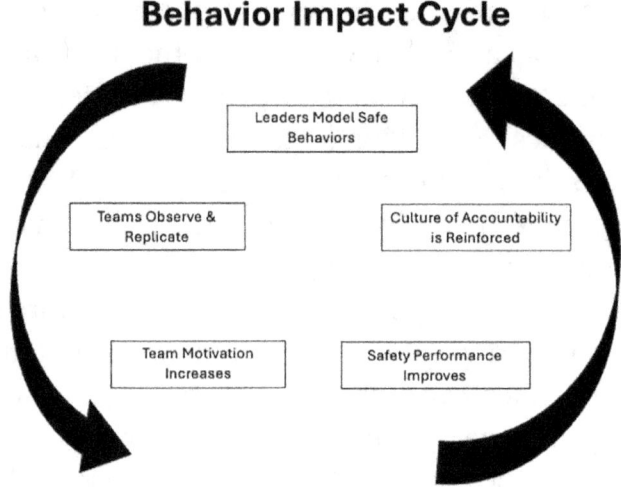

Perform Safety Tasks Publicly: Before your team, conduct routine safety checks or equipment inspections to show that these tasks are essential and non-negotiable.

Engage in Safety Conversations: Talk to your workers about safety as you observe them on the job. Ask about any hazards they've noticed or whether they've identified new risks. These conversations reinforce the importance of ongoing hazard identification.

Be Consistent—Even in Challenging Situations

One of the most critical moments to model behavior is during high-pressure situations, such as when deadlines are tight or when equipment needs rapid repair.

- **Avoid Cutting Corners:** Workers look to their leaders for cues on how to proceed when the pressure is on. If you skip a step or ignore safety protocols, they'll assume it's acceptable. Instead, take a moment to regroup, reassess risks, and follow the proper procedures, even if it means slowing down.
- **Reinforce Standards in Emergencies:** It's easy to let safety standards slip during emergency repair work. However, this is when modeling behavior becomes most critical. As a leader, you must ensure that no one rushes into a dangerous situation without proper safeguards in place.

Example: A utility company supervisor, under pressure to restore power after a severe storm, took the time to ensure that all necessary grounding procedures were followed before repairs began, even though it delayed the job. His refusal to bypass safety steps reinforced the company's commitment to safety, and his team later expressed gratitude for prioritizing their well-being over speed.

Participate in Safety Training and Briefings

Safety training and briefings shouldn't just be for the rank-and-file workers. Leaders who actively participate in these sessions demonstrate that safety is a shared responsibility.

Attend and Engage in Training

Attend safety training sessions alongside your team and ask questions. Your participation emphasizes the importance of continuous learning.

Lead by Example in Briefings

When conducting pre-job safety briefings, take the time to review key hazards, PPE requirements, and safe work practices. Workers will take these briefings more seriously if they see you leading with conviction.

Visualized Checklist for Safety Briefings:

- Have you reviewed today's hazards with your team?
- Did you confirm that all PPE and tools are in working order?
- Have all crew members acknowledged and understood their roles?

When Mistakes Happen: How to Handle It

No leader is perfect, and there will be times when even the best safety practices are overlooked. What matters most is how you, as a leader, handle these situations. When you make a mistake or witness unsafe behavior, it's crucial to address it in a way that reinforces safety standards without alienating your team.

- **Admit Your Own Mistakes:** If you slip up and fail to follow a safety procedure, acknowledge it openly. This demonstrates humility and accountability and shows your team that everyone is responsible for maintaining safety—no exceptions.
- **Use the Mistake as a Learning Opportunity:** Turn your misstep into a teachable moment for the team. Discuss what went wrong and how it could have been prevented.
- **Recommit to Safety:** Reinforce that safety is a continuous process, and even leaders need to refocus from time to time.

Example: A safety manager skipped an inspection step while rushing to get a transformer back online. Realizing his mistake, he gathered the crew, admitted the error, and explained why the missed step was crucial for preventing equipment failure. His openness encouraged the crew to share their own observations about potential hazards, creating a more collaborative safety culture.

Correct Unsafe Behaviors Immediately

When you observe unsafe behavior in your team, address it immediately—but do so constructively. Public shaming or reprimanding can create a culture of fear rather than one of safety.

Address the Issue Privately: Pull the individual aside to discuss what you observed and why it's a concern. Offer suggestions for improvement and clarify that your goal is to keep them safe.

Follow-up: Later, check in with the individual to ensure they adopt safer behaviors. Reinforce the positive changes you see.

Example: A supervisor noticed a lineman working without proper gloves during maintenance. Instead of berating him before the team, the supervisor asked him privately if he knew the PPE requirement. The lineman admitted he was rushing and forgot. The supervisor took the opportunity to remind him of the risks and thanked him for correcting the behavior without further incident.

The Ripple Effect of Modeling Behavior

The behaviors you model don't just influence your immediate team—they ripple out to the entire organization. When safety-conscious leadership becomes part of the culture, it impacts:

- **New Employees:** New hires quickly adapt to the behaviors they see modeled by their supervisors and peers. If they enter an environment where safety is visibly prioritized, they're more likely to adopt those same habits.

Modeling the Behavior You Seek

- **Other Leaders:** Your example influences how other leaders manage their teams. When you demonstrate that safety is a non-negotiable part of leadership, other supervisors are more likely to follow suit, leading to a safer organization as a whole.

Example: At a contracting company, one manager was known for conducting detailed safety audits on his projects, which resulted in very few incidents. His approach became a standard practice across the company, as other managers saw the value in modeling that behavior. Within a year, the entire company saw a significant drop in reportable incidents due to this shift in leadership practices.

Tips for Modeling Safe Behaviors

- **Be Consistent**: Your team will follow your lead, so ensure you model safe behaviors daily—not just when convenient.
- **Encourage Peer Accountability**: Foster an environment where workers feel comfortable reminding each other of safety protocols. Lead by example by openly accepting feedback about your own behavior.
- **Make Safety a Core Value**: Consistently communicate that safety is not a task but a company's core value. Emphasize this during briefings, reviews, and informal conversations.

- **Recognize Good Behavior:** When you see someone on your team modeling your desired behavior, acknowledge it. This reinforces positive actions and encourages others to follow suit.

Conclusion

Modeling the behavior you want to see in your team is one of the most effective ways to establish and maintain a strong safety culture. You create an environment where safety is ingrained in daily operations by consistently demonstrating safe practices, engaging with your team, and handling mistakes with transparency. Remember, your team will mirror your actions, so make sure you're setting the right example every step of the way.

The next chapter will explore the power of mentoring in developing a safety-conscious workforce and how you can guide individuals to take personal responsibility for their safety and the safety of others.

Chapter 6

The Power of Mentoring in Building a Safety-First Culture

Introduction

Mentoring is vital in creating and sustaining a safety-first culture, especially in high-risk industries like powerline electrical work. It goes beyond simply teaching procedures—mentoring is about cultivating the right mindset and helping less experienced workers navigate the complexities of the job while prioritizing safety above all else. A good mentor doesn't just impart knowledge but also instills a sense of personal accountability and confidence in their mentees.

This chapter will explore why mentoring is crucial for developing a safety-first mindset, how it impacts safety performance, and practical steps to establish effective mentoring relationships in your organization. Through mentoring, leaders ensure that safety practices are understood and deeply embedded into every worker's daily routines and behaviors.

Why Mentoring is Critical in the Electrical Utility Industry

The electrical utility industry presents a unique set of challenges that demand not only technical expertise but also an unwavering commitment to safety. Mentoring plays an essential role in shaping how workers approach their daily tasks, helping them recognize and mitigate risks that aren't always immediately apparent.

Here's why mentoring is indispensable in this field:

- **Transferring Knowledge and Experience:** No matter how much training a worker receives in the classroom, there is no substitute for the practical, on-the-job experience that only a seasoned mentor can provide. Mentors pass down lessons learned from years of working in the field, helping newer workers avoid the same mistakes.
- **Cultivating Safe Habits:** Safety habits are not formed overnight. Mentors ensure that their mentees consistently practice safe work habits, reinforcing these behaviors through repetition and guidance. Over time, these practices become second nature.
- **Confidence Building:** New workers may lack the confidence to assert themselves or make safety decisions under pressure. A mentor helps build that confidence by providing a supportive

environment where the mentee can ask questions, make mistakes, and learn without fear of judgment.

Example: Consider a scenario where an apprentice is working on a pole installation for the first time. The mentor walks them through each step, pointing out the hazards and explaining why certain safety measures are critical. This guidance not only helps the apprentice understand the procedure but also instills the importance of vigilance, which will stick with them long after the mentoring period.

How Mentoring Improves Safety Performance

Mentoring has a direct impact on safety performance, as it helps workers develop both the technical skills and the mindset required to maintain high safety standards. Here's how effective mentoring improves safety outcomes:

Encourages Proactive Risk Management

Mentors teach their mentees to look for potential hazards and take steps to mitigate them before they become serious risks. This proactive approach prevents accidents by encouraging workers to stay ahead of potential dangers.

A good mentor will constantly ask the mentee questions like:

- "What could go wrong in this situation?"
- "Have you considered all the risks?"
- "What can we do to make this task safer?"

By encouraging this type of thinking, mentors help their men develop the habit of assessing risks before taking action.

Reinforces the Importance of Procedures

While it may be tempting to cut corners when under pressure, mentors teach their mentees that following safety procedures is non-negotiable, through daily guidance and correction, mentors reinforce the importance of sticking to protocols, even when it might slow down the work.

Example: During an emergency response to a downed line, a mentor observes their mentee rushing through the safety checks. The mentor steps in, reminding the mentee that safety must come first, even in urgent situations. This interaction reinforces the idea that no deadline or emergency is worth compromising safety.

Builds Long-Term Safety Habits

Mentoring focuses on repetition and reinforcement. As mentees repeat tasks under the watchful eye of a mentor, they begin to internalize safety procedures. Over time, these practices become ingrained habits that will persist even after the mentoring period ends.

Visualized Checklist for Safety Habits

1. **Pre-Job Planning:**
   - Have we identified all hazards?
   - Is the appropriate PPE in use?
2. **During the Task:**
   - Are we adhering to the work plan and safety protocols?
   - Are we communicating effectively as a team?
3. **Post-Job Review:**
   - What went well, and what can be improved?
   - Were any safety protocols overlooked, and why?

Key Elements of Effective Mentoring

To maximize the benefits of mentoring, it's essential to approach it with structure and intent. Here are the key elements of an effective mentoring relationship:

Establish Clear Goals and Expectations

At the beginning of the mentoring relationship, the mentor and mentee should clearly understand the objectives. This ensures that both parties stay focused on safety and skill development. Common goals might include:

- Understanding specific safety protocols.
- Improving hazard identification skills.
- Developing confidence in making safety decisions.

By setting clear goals, the mentor and mentee can measure progress and adjust their approach as needed.

Example: A mentor and apprentice might set a goal for the apprentice to lead a safety briefing within three months. Leading the briefing will require the apprentice to understand and explain safety protocols, reinforcing their learning.

Encourage Two-Way Communication

Mentoring is a two-way street. While the mentor provides guidance, the mentee should also feel empowered to ask questions and voice concerns. Open communication helps build trust and ensures that safety concerns are addressed in real-time.

- **Ask for Feedback:** Mentors should regularly ask their mentees for feedback. This could be about the mentoring process itself or about specific safety practices.
- **Offer Constructive Feedback:** Focus on solutions rather than criticism when providing feedback. This helps the mentee feel supported rather than judged, making them more receptive to guidance.

Example: After a job, a mentor might ask their mentee, "How do you think that went? Were there any safety concerns you noticed?" This encourages the mentee to reflect on their actions and think.

Lead by Example

Mentors must model the behavior they expect from their mentees. If the mentor cuts corners or ignores safety protocols, the mentee will likely follow suit. Leading by example means consistently adhering to safety protocols and demonstrating a commitment to doing the job correctly every time.

Pro Tip: When performing a task, talk through your actions and explain the safety considerations behind them. This reinforces the procedure and gives the mentee insight into your thought process.

Mentoring in High-Pressure Environments

The electrical utility industry is no stranger to high-pressure situations like storm recovery or urgent repairs. Mentoring is especially important in these scenarios, where the temptation to rush can lead to dangerous mistakes.

Handling Stress and Pressure

A key part of mentoring is teaching workers how to maintain composure under pressure. This involves:

- **Demonstrating Calm Decision-Making:** Mentors should model calm, clear decision-making during stressful situations. By staying focused and not letting the pressure dictate their actions, mentors show their mentees how to keep safety at the top of their minds, even when the stakes are high.
- **Reinforcing Safe Practices:** Mentors must remind their mentees that speed should never come at the cost of safety. Even in emergency situations, all safety protocols should be followed to the letter.

Example: During a storm, a mentor notices the crew trying to work too quickly to restore power. The mentor gathers the team, calmly reiterates the safety procedures, and ensures everyone follows the correct protocols before work continues. This reinforces that no job is too urgent to compromise safety.

Common Challenges in Mentoring and How to Overcome Them

Mentoring, especially in safety-critical industries, comes with its own set of challenges. Here are some common issues and how to address them:

- **Resistance to Feedback:** Sometimes, mentees may resist feedback, especially if they're used to working in a certain way or if they don't fully appreciate the risks involved. Overcoming this challenge requires patience and a constructive approach.
- **Frame Feedback Positively:** Rather than focusing on what the mentee did wrong, frame feedback in terms of how they can improve and why it matters for their safety. Emphasize that the goal is to help them become a better, safer worker.
- **Time Constraints:** Mentoring takes time, and it may feel like there's never enough of it in a busy work environment. However, safety cannot be compromised, and mentoring must be prioritized to develop a competent, safety-focused workforce.
- **Integrate Mentoring into Daily Tasks:** Instead of setting aside time specifically for mentoring, look for opportunities to mentor throughout the day.

Every task is a learning opportunity, and mentors can offer guidance during routine work without detracting from productivity.

Building a Mentoring Culture

To make mentoring a cornerstone of your safety program, building a culture where mentoring is seen as a continuous, long-term investment in the workforce is important. Here's how:

- **Formalize Mentorship:** Create structured mentoring programs that pair less-experienced workers with veteran mentors. Ensure that mentoring is built into new hires' onboarding process and continues as workers advance in their careers.
- **Celebrate Successes:** When mentees demonstrate significant progress in safety performance, recognize it. Publicly acknowledging mentors and mentees helps reinforce the value of mentoring and motivates others to participate in the program.

Example: A utility company set up a formal mentoring program, pairing each new hire with a mentor for the first six months. The mentor-mentee pairs were regularly reviewed to ensure progress and shared success stories across the organization. This helped to create a culture where mentoring became a valued part of everyday operations.

Conclusion

Mentoring is a powerful tool for developing a safety-conscious workforce in the electrical utility industry. Through hands-on guidance, feedback, and consistent reinforcement of safe practices, mentors help their mentees build the skills and confidence needed to work safely in even the most high-risk environments. As mentoring becomes ingrained in the company culture, it ensures that safety practices are passed down from generation to generation, ultimately creating a safer, more effective workforce.

In the next chapter, we will explore **building strong relationships** in the workplace, focusing on how trust and collaboration lead to a safer and more cohesive team.

Chapter 7

Building Strong Relationships for a Safer Workplace

Introduction

In high-risk industries like powerline electrical work, safety relies not just on protocols and procedures but also on the strength of the relationships within a team. Safety culture is inherently people-centered, and strong relationships enable better communication, trust, accountability, and collaboration. When workers trust each other and their supervisors, communicate effectively, and feel a shared responsibility for safety, the entire team functions more efficiently, making accidents less likely.

This chapter explores the role of building strong relationships in fostering a safety-conscious environment. We will delve into how trust, communication, collaboration, and accountability form the foundation of a safe workplace and provide practical tips for strengthening these connections within your team.

The Role of Relationships in Safety

In the electrical utility industry, where hazards are omnipresent, and mistakes can have severe consequences, the quality of relationships within a team directly affects safety outcomes. Strong relationships between coworkers and between workers and supervisors create an environment where safety becomes a shared value rather than just a set of rules to follow.

Why Relationships Matter in High-Risk Environments

Workers in high-risk environments like powerline electrical work must rely on one another to maintain safety. Whether spotting hazards, ensuring safety procedures are followed, or providing backup in emergencies, a team's effectiveness hinges on how well its members can communicate and trust each other.

- **Trust:** Workers who trust each other are empowered to share concerns, point out unsafe behaviors, and offer assistance without hesitation, knowing that their input is valued and can make a difference.
- **Communication:** Clear and open communication provides a sense of security, ensuring that all team members understand the risks, the plan,

and their roles in keeping the job safe, thereby boosting their confidence in their tasks.
- **Accountability:** Workers who feel responsible not just for their own safety but also for the safety of their colleagues are more likely to hold each other accountable.

Example: A seasoned lineman and a new apprentice worked together on a routine line replacement. The apprentice noticed an unusual vibration in the line but hesitated to say anything because he wasn't sure it was significant. Sensing the apprentice's hesitation, the lineman encouraged him to speak up. Upon inspection, they found that a support clamp was loose and could have caused a serious incident. The strong relationship between the two workers—based on trust and open communication—prevented a potential accident.

Building Trust to Strengthen Safety

Trust is the foundation of any effective team. In the context of safety, trust enables workers to rely on each other, speak up about concerns, and feel confident that their teammates are prioritizing safety. Workers may hesitate to voice concerns without trust, leading to dangerous situations.

Trust Among Coworkers

Trust between team members is essential in ensuring everyone looks out for each other. When workers trust each other, they are more likely to:

- **Communicate Freely:** Openly discuss safety concerns without fear of judgment or reprimand.
- **Act on Concerns:** Workers who trust their teammates are more likely to act when something seems unsafe, whether by addressing the issue directly or reporting it to a supervisor.
- **Help Each Other:** Strong trust leads to a greater willingness to help colleagues follow safety procedures, ensuring no one cuts corners, even in high-pressure situations.

Trust Between Workers and Supervisors

Trust between workers and supervisors is just as important. Workers must trust that their supervisors will support them in prioritizing safety, even when it means slowing down or taking extra precautions.

- **Consistency:** Supervisors who consistently follow safety protocols and encourage their teams to do the same build trust over time. Workers know they can always rely on their leaders to prioritize safety.

- **Transparency:** When supervisors are transparent about safety issues and share lessons from past incidents, it reinforces that safety is a shared priority, not just a box to check off.
- **Fairness:** Workers are more likely to report safety issues when they know that concerns will be taken seriously and handled fairly, without fear of blame or punishment.

Example: At one utility company, a lineman raised concerns about a faulty safety harness during a safety briefing. The supervisor immediately stopped the job, inspected the equipment, and ensured replacements were provided. By taking swift, decisive action, the supervisor reinforced trust within the team. Workers knew their safety concerns were a priority, and they were more likely to report potential hazards in the future.

The Importance of Clear Communication for Safety

Effective communication is essential in any job, but it can be the difference between life and death in a high-risk environment. Clear, direct communication ensures that all team members understand their roles, the risks involved, and the steps they must take to stay safe.

Open and Honest Communication

Open communication is a key element of a strong safety culture. Workers must feel comfortable voicing concerns, asking questions, and offering feedback on safety practices. Leaders should actively encourage this type of communication by creating an environment where safety discussions are not just welcome but expected.

- **Regular Safety Briefings:** Pre-job briefings should always include time for workers to raise safety concerns or point out potential hazards.
- **Two-Way Dialogue:** Safety communication should not be one-sided. Leaders should ask for input from the team and genuinely consider their feedback.

Example: A contracting company noticed workers often hesitated to speak up during safety briefings. To address this, the company introduced a practice where, at the end of every briefing, each crew member was required to identify one potential safety risk related to the day's work. This simple change fostered a more open dialogue and helped workers engage more in hazard identification.

Communicating During High-Risk Tasks

Clear communication becomes even more critical in fast-paced, high-risk situations. Workers must be able to convey important information quickly to their teammates and supervisors without ambiguity.

- **Use Clear and Direct Language:** Avoid vague terms, especially during emergencies. Be specific about what must happen and who is responsible for each action.
- **Confirm Understanding:** Don't assume everyone has understood the instructions—ask team members to repeat key points to ensure clarity.

Example: During a storm restoration job, a crew leader was concerned that the high winds could complicate the operation. He clearly communicated the plan, assigning specific roles and emphasizing the need for each team member to repeat their tasks aloud before execution. This process ensured everyone understood their responsibilities, preventing miscommunication and accidents during the job.

The Role of Collaboration in a Safety Culture

Collaboration is essential for communication. When workers collaborate effectively, they create an environment where safety is a shared responsibility. No one works in isolation, and every team member looks out for the safety of their coworkers.

Fostering a Team-First Mentality

In a collaborative environment, safety isn't just an individual concern—it's a team effort. Workers should be encouraged to actively participate in keeping the workplace safe by:

- **Watching Out for Each Other:** Workers who see a colleague about to make an unsafe move should feel empowered to speak up. This is not about criticizing but about protecting one another.
- **Offering Help:** Team members should be quick to offer assistance when a job requires an extra set of hands or when someone is struggling to complete a task safely.

Example: During a pole installation job, one worker noticed a fellow crew member struggling to secure a line in windy conditions. Instead of ignoring it, he stepped in to help instead of ignoring it, ensuring the line was secured properly before continuing with his work. This type of collaboration not only prevents accidents but also strengthens team bonds.

Involving Everyone in Safety Solutions

Regarding safety improvements, the best ideas often come from the workers who are directly involved in the tasks. Encourage all team members, regardless of their experience level, to contribute ideas for making the job safer.

- **Value Diverse Perspectives:** New workers might bring fresh insights that experienced workers haven't considered. At the same time, seasoned veterans can share practical solutions based on years of experience.
- **Encourage Innovation:** If a worker suggests a new tool, technique, or approach to improve safety, consider it seriously. Creating an atmosphere where innovation is welcomed encourages a proactive approach to safety.

Example: A group of apprentices working on a job noticed that the existing method for inspecting certain powerline components required precarious positioning. They proposed a new tool to streamline the process and make it safer. After testing the new method, the team found it improved both safety and efficiency, highlighting the value of encouraging contributions from everyone.

Accountability: A Key Element in Strong Team Relationships

Accountability is crucial to a safety-first mindset. When workers feel accountable not only for their own safety but also for the safety of their colleagues, they are more likely to follow safety protocols and encourage others to do the same.

Creating a Culture of Accountability

Workers must understand that safety isn't just a set of rules—it's a personal responsibility. Each worker must hold themselves accountable for the following procedures, using PPE, and adhering to safety protocols, but they should also feel empowered to hold their teammates accountable.

- **Promote Mutual Accountability:** Encourage workers to remind each other to follow safety protocols respectfully. This could be as simple as pointing out when someone forgets to wear their PPE or alerting a colleague to an overlooked hazard.
- **Address Unsafe Behavior:** When unsafe behavior is observed, it should be corrected immediately, but the correction should be constructive. Instead of blaming or criticizing, focus on improving the behavior to prevent future incidents.

Example: During a routine job, a worker noticed that his colleague hadn't properly secured a ladder before climbing it. He immediately pointed it out, and they fixed the issue together. The crew leader later praised the worker for speaking up, reinforcing the culture of mutual accountability.

Building Long-term Relationships for Sustained Safety

Strong relationships improve safety in the short term and contribute to sustained safety performance over time. When teams are built on trust, communication, collaboration, and accountability, they are better equipped to handle both routine tasks and high-stress situations.

Investing in Relationship Building

Leaders should view relationship building as an ongoing investment. Whether through regular safety briefings, team-building exercises, or simply fostering a supportive work environment, these efforts pay off by creating a cohesive team prioritizing safety.

- **Regular Team Check-Ins:** Periodic check-ins, both one-on-one and as a group, help strengthen relationships. These meetings provide opportunities for workers to share feedback and for leaders to reinforce the importance of safety.
- **Recognizing Safe Behaviors:** Recognize and reward workers who demonstrate strong safety practices through verbal praise or more formal recognition. This not only encourages safe behaviors but also reinforces the value of teamwork.

Example: At a large utility company, crews that consistently demonstrated high safety performance were recognized during monthly safety meetings. The company tried to publicly celebrate workers who stepped up to help a colleague or identified a potential hazard. This recognition reinforced the idea that safety was a shared responsibility and helped foster stronger relationships among team members.

Conclusion

Strong relationships are at the heart of a safe workplace. Trust, communication, collaboration, and accountability are essential elements that allow teams to work together effectively and ensure that safety remains the top priority. In the electrical utility industry, where risks are high and the consequences of mistakes can be severe, building these relationships is not just important—it's essential.

By investing in these relationships, workers and leaders create an environment where safety becomes a shared value, and everyone looks out for one another. In the next chapter, we will explore the role of **safety tools and checklists** in standardizing safety practices and ensuring consistency across teams.

Chapter 8

Implementing Safety Tools and Checklists for Consistency and Accountability

Introduction

Safety in the electrical utility industry cannot rely solely on individual vigilance and team relationships. It requires a structured, systematic approach to ensure consistency across teams and tasks. **Safety tools and checklists** are vital in achieving this. They standardize procedures, help workers remember critical steps, and ensure nothing is overlooked, even under high-pressure or routine conditions. When used effectively, these tools serve as a safety net, preventing human error and reinforcing a culture of accountability.

This chapter will focus on the importance of safety tools and checklists, how they enhance safety performance and practical ways to implement them across your organization. We will explore how these tools help streamline processes, reduce accidents, and ensure compliance with safety standards.

The Role of Safety Tools and Checklists in Reducing Human Error

In high-risk industries like powerline electrical work, even the most experienced workers can overlook critical safety steps, particularly when they are dealing with time pressure, fatigue, or a false sense of routine. This is where safety tools and checklists come in—they help eliminate human error by providing a structured process for completing tasks.

Checklists as a Safety Net

Checklists serve as a critical safety net, ensuring that each step of a job is completed properly and in the correct sequence. They take the guesswork out of high-risk tasks, especially in situations where complacency might otherwise set in.

- **Consistency Across Teams:** When everyone follows the same checklist, safety standards are maintained across different crews and locations, ensuring consistency in task performance.
- **Reducing Cognitive Load:** Checklists help reduce cognitive overload by providing a step-by-step guide for workers, even in stressful or complex situations.

Example: During a pole replacement job, a team used a detailed pre-task checklist to verify all equipment, including fall protection and grounding, was correctly set up before beginning the job. The checklist prevented a potential oversight when one team member realized his harness had not been inspected. This simple tool likely prevented a serious injury and reinforced the team's adherence to safety standards.

Types of Safety Tools and Checklists for the Electrical Utility Industry

Different tasks require different tools, and the electrical utility industry has many safety-critical processes that can benefit from tailored checklists and tools. Let's examine a few key types of safety tools and how they can be applied to improve performance and minimize risks.

Pre-Job Briefing Checklists

Pre-job briefing checklists help ensure all necessary preparations are made before work begins. They provide a framework for discussing potential hazards, assigning roles, and confirming that safety protocols are understood by everyone involved.

- **Hazard Identification:** A checklist prompts workers to consider site-specific hazards, such as weather conditions, nearby energized lines, or equipment issues.

- **Equipment Checks:** Before starting the job, ensure that all necessary tools and personal protective equipment (PPE) are inspected and in good working order.

Visualized Pre-Job Checklist Example:

1. Identify and discuss site-specific hazards.
2. Verify that all workers are wearing appropriate PPE.
3. Confirm that all tools and equipment have been inspected.
4. Review emergency procedures and exit routes.
5. Assign and confirm roles for the day's tasks.

Task-Specific Checklists

Task-specific checklists focus on individual job steps that must be followed in order to ensure safety. These can be customized for tasks like line repairs, pole installations, or equipment inspections.

- **Line Repair Checklist:** This might include steps such as isolating the line, testing for voltage, grounding the equipment, and ensuring all PPE is in place.
- **Pole Installation Checklist:** These steps could include soil testing, verifying pole alignment, ensuring structural support, and conducting fall protection checks before climbing.

Example: A crew performing a complex line re-energization used a task-specific checklist to ensure all safety protocols were followed. The team leader checked off each step, reducing the chance of missing a critical task. Midway through, the checklist reminded the crew to confirm that grounding had been double-checked, catching a potential error that could have led to an arc flash.

Emergency Response Checklists

In emergency situations, there is no room for error or delay. Emergency response checklists ensure that everyone knows their role, that communication is clear, and that safety protocols are strictly followed.

- **Storm Recovery Checklist:** This checklist could include steps like assessing the condition of equipment, identifying damaged infrastructure, assigning roles for hazard mitigation, and ensuring safe access to work areas.
- **Accident Response Checklist:** When an incident occurs, an accident response checklist ensures that the situation is managed correctly, from securing the site to administering first aid and notifying the necessary authorities.

Example: During a storm recovery operation, an emergency response checklist guided the crew through critical steps to restore power safely. Despite the chaotic environment, the checklist helped keep everyone on task, ensuring that hazards like downed lines and flooded areas were managed safely before repairs began.

How Safety Tools Reinforce Accountability

Safety tools and checklists are not just about following steps but also about creating a culture of accountability where everyone is responsible for completing tasks safely and consistently. By implementing these tools, leaders ensure that every worker understands and takes ownership of their role in maintaining a safe work environment.

Accountability Through Documentation

One of the most important aspects of using safety checklists is the documentation that comes with them. When workers are required to sign off on each step, it creates a tangible record of their accountability.

- **Sign-Offs for Task Completion:** Having workers sign off on each completed checklist step reinforces their responsibility to ensure the task was completed safely. This also provides a documented trail, which is essential for audits or investigations.
- **Shared Responsibility:** Checklists are often completed as a team, reinforcing the idea that safety

is a shared responsibility. Everyone must be involved in confirming that each step has been properly executed.

Enhancing Supervisor Oversight

Safety tools also enable supervisors to oversee tasks more effectively. When checklists are in place, supervisors can easily review whether all required safety steps were followed, ensuring no shortcuts were taken. This oversight adds an extra layer of accountability for both workers and leaders.

- **Spot-Checking Checklists:** Supervisors should regularly review completed checklists to ensure compliance and provide feedback. This not only reinforces the checklist's importance but also helps identify areas where additional training or clarification might be needed.
- **Using Data to Improve Safety:** Documented checklists provide valuable data that can be used to identify trends, improve training, or adjust procedures based on real-world experience. By analyzing completed checklists, supervisors can spot and proactively address recurring issues.

Example: A supervisor at a contracting company noticed that workers frequently skipped certain steps in the equipment inspection checklist, leading to minor equipment failures. After reviewing the data, he implemented additional training and redesigned the checklist to clarify those steps. This simple change resulted in fewer equipment failures and improved overall safety compliance.

Implementing Safety Tools and Checklists Across Your Organization

Safety tools and checklists must be consistently integrated into every aspect of your operation to fully leverage their benefits. Here are some practical steps for implementing these tools effectively.

Customizing Tools for Your Specific Needs

Every organization and job site has its own unique set of risks and challenges. It's important to customize safety tools and checklists to reflect these realities. Off-the-shelf checklists can be a great starting point, but they should be tailored to fit your specific tasks, equipment, and working conditions.

- **Involve Workers in the Process:** Workers are often the best source of insight into the specific hazards they face. Involve them in the development of checklists to ensure that the tools are practical and relevant to their work.
- **Update Regularly:** Safety procedures and tools should evolve based on new information,

technologies, and lessons learned from past incidents. Review and update your checklists regularly to keep them current and effective.

Training Workers on the Importance of Checklists

Checklists and safety tools are only effective if workers understand how and why to use them. Training is essential to ensure that workers don't view checklists as just another formality but as crucial to keeping themselves and their colleagues safe.

- **Hands-On Training:** Incorporate checklist usage into practical, hands-on training. Show workers how to integrate the tools into their daily routines and explain the reasons behind each step on the checklist.
- **Reinforce During Safety Meetings:** Use safety meetings to review the importance of checklists and address any concerns or questions workers may have. Encourage workers to share their experiences with checklists and how they've helped prevent accidents.

Making Safety Tools Easily Accessible

For checklists and safety tools to be used consistently, they must be easily accessible to workers. This could mean providing digital versions via tablets or smartphones or ensuring printed checklists are available on-site.

- **Digital Tools:** Many organizations are moving towards digital checklists, which can streamline the process and make it easier to track compliance. Digital tools also allow real-time updates and integration with other safety management systems.
- **Hard Copies:** Printed checklists may still be the most practical option for teams working in remote or challenging environments. Ensure that hard copies are readily available and easy to use, even in tough conditions.

The Long-Term Benefits of Using Safety Tools and Checklists

Integrating safety tools and checklists into your daily operations leads to long-term benefits for both workers and the organization as a whole. These tools:

- **Reduce Incidents:** Checklists directly reduce the likelihood of accidents and injuries by standardizing safety processes and eliminating room for error.
- **Improve Efficiency:** When workers know exactly what to do and when to do it, tasks are completed more efficiently and with fewer disruptions.

- **Promote a Culture of Safety:** Consistent use of safety tools reinforces the importance of safety throughout the organization, helping to create a culture where safety is second nature to everyone.

Examples of Safety Checklists

1. Pre-Job Briefing Checklist
This checklist ensures that the team is aligned on potential hazards, roles, and safety protocols before any task begins.

Pre-Job Briefing Checklist	Status	Comments
1. Identify and discuss site-specific hazards.	☐ Yes	
2. Verify all team members are wearing appropriate PPE.	☐ Yes	
3. Inspect tools and equipment for functionality.	☐ Yes	
4. Confirm grounding and lockout/tagout procedures.	☐ Yes	
5. Review the work plan, including individual roles.	☐ Yes	
6. Discuss environmental conditions (weather, terrain).	☐ Yes	
7. Review the emergency response plan and nearest exit.	☐ Yes	
8. Confirm all team members understand the safety steps.	☐ Yes	

Implementing Safety Tools and Checklists

How to Use: Each item must be checked and verified before work starts. The team leader should facilitate the discussion, and every worker should participate to ensure all risks are identified and understood.

2. Task-Specific Checklist: Line Repair

This checklist is tailored for line repair tasks. It ensures that each step is followed in the correct sequence to avoid safety hazards.

Line Repair Checklist	Status	Comments
1. Verify line de-energization and lockout/tagout.	☐ Yes	
2. Test the line for residual voltage before proceeding.	☐ Yes	
3. Apply grounding procedures.	☐ Yes	
4. Inspect harnesses and fall protection systems.	☐ Yes	
5. Verify the structural stability of poles and supports.	☐ Yes	
6. Use insulated tools and PPE during repairs.	☐ Yes	
7. Confirm communication protocols are in place.	☐ Yes	
8. Complete post-repair voltage testing.	☐ Yes	
9. Remove grounds and re-energize the line.	☐ Yes	

How to Use: This checklist ensures that all critical safety steps are followed before proceeding with any repair task. The team leader must verify each task, and workers must confirm completion before moving on.

3. Storm Recovery Checklist (Emergency Response)

This checklist ensures that all hazards are identified during storm recovery efforts and that the crew's safety is prioritized in the chaotic environment.

Storm Recovery Checklist	Status	Comments
1. Assess the condition of the site (fallen lines, poles).	☐ Yes	
2. Identify potential electrical and environmental hazards.	☐ Yes	
3. Verify the de-energization of lines and use of lockout/tagout.	☐ Yes	
4. Establish clear communication protocols.	☐ Yes	
5. Confirm access to emergency medical supplies.	☐ Yes	
6. Assign roles for hazard mitigation and equipment recovery.	☐ Yes	
7. Secure the work area and set up barricades if necessary.	☐ Yes	
8. Perform tool and PPE inspections before work starts.	☐ Yes	
9. Monitor environmental changes (e.g., wind, lightning).	☐ Yes	

Implementing Safety Tools and Checklists

How to Use: This checklist is designed for chaotic or emergency environments, ensuring that the team systematically addresses hazards. The supervisor leads the checklist process, while workers focus on safety before engaging in recovery activities.

4. Equipment Inspection Checklist

This checklist ensures that all equipment is in good working condition before use, preventing potential failures and accidents.

Equipment Inspection Checklist	Status	Comments
1. Inspect fall protection harnesses for wear and damage.	☐ Yes	
2. Inspect ropes, slings, and pulleys for fraying.	☐ Yes	
3. Check that hand tools are free from defects or damage.	☐ Yes	
4. Verify insulated tools are functional and undamaged.	☐ Yes	
5. Test voltage testers and grounding equipment.	☐ Yes	
6. Ensure ladder and scaffold stability and integrity.	☐ Yes	
7. Inspect trucks and heavy equipment for mechanical issues.	☐ Yes	
8. Confirm fire extinguishers and first aid kits are stocked and functional.	☐ Yes	

How to Use: Conduct equipment inspections before every job. Document any equipment failures or issues and address them before proceeding with work.

5. Emergency Response Checklist

This checklist is a crucial tool that ensures the team is well-prepared to respond quickly and efficiently to any on-the-job emergency, instilling a sense of preparedness and confidence in the crew. It minimizes risk and protects the crew by providing a structured approach to emergency response.

Emergency Response Checklist	Status	Comments
1. Confirm the location of emergency contact numbers.	☐ Yes	
2. Ensure access to first aid kits and medical supplies.	☐ Yes	
3. Review emergency evacuation procedures.	☐ Yes	
4. Verify the nearest emergency exits or meeting points.	☐ Yes	
5. Assign roles in case of an emergency (who calls, who provides aid).	☐ Yes	
6. Ensure all crew members are aware of emergency procedures.	☐ Yes	

How to Use: This checklist should be completed at the start of each job to prepare the crew for emergencies.

Supervisors should review it with the team and assign specific roles to respond effectively in a crisis.

6. Post-Job Review Checklist

After a job is complete, this checklist plays a vital role in ensuring that the site is properly secured and that lessons from the job can be used to improve future safety performance.

Post-Job Review Checklist	Status	Comments
1. Confirm all tools and equipment have been safely stored.	☐ Yes	
2. Ensure the site is clear of debris and hazards.	☐ Yes	
3. Review any incidents, near misses, or unexpected hazards.	☐ Yes	
4. Conduct a team debrief to identify improvements for future jobs.	☐ Yes	
5. Verify that all equipment inspections and safety checks are complete.	☐ Yes	
6. Secure the job site before leaving (e.g., lockout/tagout remains, barricades).	☐ Yes	

How to Use: This checklist helps the team wrap up the job safely and provides an opportunity to reflect on lessons learned. It should be used after every job to ensure no loose ends are left on-site.

Conclusion

Safety tools and checklists are essential for maintaining consistency and accountability in high-risk industries like powerline electrical work. They provide a structured approach to safety, helping teams prevent errors, manage hazards, and reinforce safe behaviors. When used effectively, these tools improve safety outcomes and create a culture where every worker feels accountable for their role in maintaining a safe work environment.

The next chapter will focus on **real-life experiences and lessons learned** from incidents in the electrical utility industry and how these stories can improve safety practices across the board.

Chapter 9

Real-Life Experiences and Lessons Learned

Introduction

The electrical utility industry is one of the most dangerous sectors, where even the smallest oversight can lead to severe injury or death. Over the years, countless incidents have provided valuable lessons, shaping the way safety is approached today. Learning from real-life experiences is critical for improving safety protocols and reinforcing a culture of vigilance and personal accountability. Every near miss, injury, and fatality teaches us something—often hard-earned lessons that must be passed on to ensure they are never repeated.

This chapter will examine real-life examples from the electrical utility industry, detailing what went wrong, the consequences, and the corrective actions taken. We will explore how these lessons have shaped current safety practices and discuss the importance of reflecting on these incidents to prevent future accidents.

Learning from Near Misses

Near misses are often seen as lucky breaks—moments when an accident almost happened but didn't. However, they are just as valuable for learning as actual incidents. Each near miss is a warning, a chance to correct behaviors and prevent a more serious incident in the future. Learning from these near misses is crucial for preventing future accidents.

The Importance of Reporting Near Misses

In some work environments, near misses go unreported because there's a tendency to downplay close calls. This can be dangerous because a near miss indicates a hazard exists, and if not addressed, it could lead to a serious incident. Reporting and analyzing near misses allows teams to identify trends and fix small issues before they escalate.

Example: In a utility company, a lineman working on a tower noticed his fall arrest system hadn't been properly secured but fortunately realized it before a fall occurred. He initially brushed it off as an oversight. However, after reporting the incident, an investigation revealed that the quick clips used on the harness were prone to misfitting, especially under extremely cold weather conditions. This near miss led to a company-wide switch to more reliable harness systems, likely preventing future fatalities.

Lesson Learned

- **Immediate Action:** Always report near misses, no matter how small they seem. Close calls provide valuable data for preventing serious accidents.
- **Equipment Updates:** Regular inspections and upgrading faulty equipment can prevent near misses from turning into injuries.

Creating a Culture of Transparency

Workers need to feel comfortable reporting near misses without fear of blame or punishment. It's essential to foster a culture where reporting is seen as a proactive step toward safety improvement, not a reflection of incompetence or failure.

- **Open Communication:** Encourage workers to share near misses openly during safety briefings or debriefs. Use these moments as teaching opportunities.
- **Non-Punitive Environment:** Make it clear that reporting a near miss will never result in punishment—only improvement.

Example: After a crew failed to report a near miss involving a miscommunication during a line re-energization, the company implemented anonymous near-miss reporting tools. Workers began to share close calls without fear of backlash, resulting in more thorough hazard assessments and stronger communication protocols.

Learning from Injuries and Fatalities

When an injury or fatality occurs, it's a tragic reminder of the dangers inherent in the job. However, these incidents also serve as a crucial learning tool for the industry. Investigating what went wrong, understanding how it could have been prevented, and sharing those lessons with others are essential for improving safety practices.

Case Study: Electrical Arc Flash Incident

Incident: A crew was performing routine maintenance on a high-voltage transformer when an electrical arc flash occurred, severely burning two workers. Upon investigation, it was discovered that one of the workers had incorrectly assumed that the equipment was de-energized without verifying with a voltage tester.

Contributing Factors

- **Complacency:** The crew had performed the task many times before, leading to overconfidence.

- **Lack of Verification:** No independent verification of de-energization using a voltage tester was conducted, a critical safety step.
- **Poor Communication:** The crew leader assumed everyone had followed the proper procedures, but this was not verified.

Corrective Actions

- **Strict Lockout/Tagout Procedures:** The company implemented more rigorous lockout/tagout verification steps, ensuring that all workers involved in a job personally verify equipment is de-energized before starting work.
- **Re-Education on Arc Flash Dangers:** Training programs were updated to reemphasize the dangers of arc flashes and the importance of PPE, such as flame-resistant clothing.
- **Pre-Job Safety Checklist:** A checklist specifically for arc flash protection was introduced, requiring all workers to acknowledge that they had followed de-energization and PPE protocols.

Lesson Learned

- **Never Assume:** Always use independent verification methods (like a voltage tester) to ensure equipment is de-energized.

- **Ongoing Training:** Regular refresher training on the dangers of arc flashes and PPE usage is essential.

Case Study: Fatal Fall from a Utility Pole

Incident: A lineman fell from a 30-foot utility pole while conducting routine line maintenance. The investigation revealed that his fall protection system had not been properly secured due to an oversight in a pre-task inspection.

Contributing Factors

- **Inadequate Fall Protection:** The worker's fall arrest harness was not properly fitted, which caused it to fail during the fall.
- **Lack of Supervision:** The crew leader had not checked the worker's equipment before the climb, assuming it had been inspected.
- **Complacency:** The worker and the crew leader had become complacent, believing the task was routine and did not require strict safety checks.

Corrective Actions

- **Mandatory PPE Checks:** The company introduced mandatory PPE checks before every climb, with the crew leader signing off on the checklist.

- **Increased Supervision:** Supervisors were required to physically inspect all workers' fall protection gear before allowing them to ascend poles or towers.
- **Enhanced Training:** The company introduced more rigorous fall protection training, with annual refresher courses to prevent complacency.

Lesson Learned

- **Routine Jobs Are Still Risky:** Even the most routine tasks carry risks and safety protocols must never be relaxed.
- **Supervision Matters:** Supervisors play a critical role in verifying that all safety equipment is properly inspected and used.

Lessons from Successful Safety Interventions

While it's important to learn from mistakes, it's equally valuable to learn from successes. There are many instances where safety interventions—like using the right equipment or adopting new safety protocols—have prevented accidents and saved lives.

Case Study: Improved Grounding Procedures Prevented Electrical Shock

Situation: A team was working on de-energizing a high-voltage transmission line. Grounding procedures were followed to prevent electrical shock, but a potential fault in the grounding system was identified during a routine inspection before any work began.

Success Factors

- **Vigilance During Inspections:** The team leader's thorough inspection of the grounding system identified a potential weak spot.
- **Commitment to Procedure:** Even though it was a routine task, the team followed grounding procedures to the letter, which prevented a major accident.
- **Team Accountability:** Every worker on the team double-checked each other's work, fostering a collaborative approach to safety.

Lesson Learned

- **Stick to Procedures, No Matter How Routine:** Even in routine operations, follow safety protocols rigorously.
- **Double-Check Critical Safety Systems:** Inspections of grounding systems or lockout/tagout procedures should always be thorough, even if no issues are immediately apparent.

Continuous Improvement: Using Lessons to Shape Future Safety

The true value of learning from real-life experiences lies in how those lessons are used to prevent future incidents. Safety is not static—it evolves based on the lessons learned from both successes and failures. Teams must continuously adapt and improve their safety procedures, using past incidents as a foundation for better performance.

Creating a System for Continuous Learning

- **Safety Debriefs After Every Job:** Make it standard practice to hold a safety debrief after each job, regardless of whether there were any incidents. This encourages workers to share near misses or potential hazards they notice.
- **Company-Wide Sharing of Lessons Learned:** Incidents and near misses should not be confined to one crew or job site. Create a system where safety lessons are shared across the entire organization to ensure everyone benefits from the learning.

Example: A utility company implemented a monthly "Safety Forum" where crews from different regions shared their most significant safety learnings from the past month, including near misses, injuries, and successful safety interventions. This improved the company's overall safety record and built a culture of continuous improvement and shared responsibility.

Integrating Technology to Improve Safety

Many of the lessons learned from real-life incidents involve updating or enhancing equipment and safety tools. Technology is increasingly important in preventing accidents, from better PPE to digital safety monitoring systems.

- **Wearable Safety Technology:** Wearable devices can monitor workers' vitals, detect falls, or alert supervisors if a worker enters a dangerous zone.
- **Digital Checklists:** Digital tools can make it easier to follow and track safety checklists, ensuring that no step is skipped and safety documentation is readily available.

Example: A contracting company introduced wearable sensors that monitor workers' heart rates and body temperatures to prevent heatstroke during outdoor summer jobs. After several near misses involving heat-related illnesses, the new technology significantly reduced these incidents by alerting workers to take breaks before they reached dangerous fatigue levels.

Incorporating Lessons into Training Programs

Every lesson learned from an incident, near miss, or safety success should be incorporated into training programs. Safety training should be dynamic, reflecting the latest industry insights and lessons from real-world experiences.

Case-Based Learning

Using real-life case studies in training makes safety concepts more relatable and memorable for workers. When workers see how a small oversight led to a major incident—or how a good decision saved lives—they reinforce the importance of safety protocols.

- **Incident Replays:** Walk workers through past incidents, using real details and outcomes to highlight the importance of following safety protocols.
- **Role-playing exercises: Allow workers to act out scenarios in which** they need to respond to a near miss or emergency, teaching them how to apply their knowledge in a practical way.

Conclusion

Real-life experiences—whether from near misses, injuries, or fatalities—offer invaluable lessons that shape the future of safety in the electrical utility industry. By analyzing incidents, sharing lessons learned, and integrating those lessons into safety protocols and training, we can prevent accidents, protect lives, and continuously improve safety standards.

Chapter 10

Sustaining a Safety Culture for the Future

Introduction

Creating a strong safety culture is a significant achievement, but maintaining and evolving that culture over time is the true challenge. The electrical utility industry is continuously changing, with new technologies, regulations, and risks emerging every day. **Sustaining a safety culture for the future** requires an ongoing commitment from everyone, from leadership to the frontline workers. It means adapting to new challenges, reinforcing key safety values, and constantly seeking ways to improve safety performance.

This final chapter will focus on how organizations can sustain and evolve their safety culture. We'll look at the strategies needed to keep safety at the forefront of operations, how to address future challenges and the role of leadership in driving long-term safety success. This chapter also covers the importance of continuous improvement, innovation, and maintaining engagement with safety as industries and technologies evolve.

The Continuous Nature of Safety Culture

Safety is not a goal that is achieved once and then forgotten. It is a continuous process that requires constant attention, reinforcement, and improvement. A strong safety culture must be adaptable to new risks, learn from past experiences, and evolve with advancements in technology, processes, and industry standards.

Treating Safety as a Dynamic Process

Safety should be viewed as an ongoing, dynamic process rather than a static set of rules. This means that safety protocols and practices must be regularly updated and adjusted to reflect changes in the workplace environment, new risks, and lessons learned from past incidents.

- **Regular Review of Safety Protocols:** Periodically review and revise safety protocols to ensure they are up-to-date with the latest regulations and best practices.
- **Encouraging Feedback:** Workers on the frontline often have valuable insights into how safety procedures can be improved. Continually solicit

feedback from workers to refine and strengthen safety practices.

Example: A contracting company discovered that their lockout/tagout procedures, while effective, were not suited for some newer, automated electrical systems. Rather than relying on outdated processes, the company updated its safety protocols to accommodate the complexities of modern equipment, improving both safety and efficiency.

Fostering a Learning Culture

A true safety culture embraces a learning mindset, where every incident, near miss, or safety success is treated as an opportunity to improve. Continuous learning ensures that the safety culture grows stronger over time and adapts to new risks and challenges.

- **Post-Incident Reviews:** Conduct thorough reviews after every incident to determine what went wrong, what could have been done differently, and how future accidents can be prevented.
- **Near-Miss Reporting:** Actively encourage near-miss reporting and treat these as improvement opportunities. Use near misses as a way to identify weak points in safety practices before a more serious incident occurs.

Leadership's Role in Sustaining a Safety Culture

Leadership is critical in sustaining a safety culture over the long term. Leadership's values, priorities, and behaviors will determine the focus and attitude toward safety across the organization. Leaders must enforce safety rules and inspire a shared commitment to safety among all employees.

Leading by Example

Leaders set the tone for safety by modeling the behaviors they expect from their teams. When leaders prioritize safety and demonstrate their commitment through actions, workers are more likely to follow suit.

- **Active Involvement in Safety:** Leaders should actively participate in safety briefings, inspections, and discussions, showing that safety is a personal priority.
- **Consistent Safety Messaging:** Leaders should consistently communicate the importance of safety, both formally through meetings and informally during day-to-day interactions with workers.

Example: A utility company CEO regularly participated in field safety inspections and toolbox talks with line workers. This visible involvement sent a strong message that safety was not just a regulatory requirement but a core value of the company's leadership. Workers responded by taking safety more seriously, resulting in fewer incidents.

Empowering Workers to Take Ownership of Safety

For safety culture to be sustained long-term, leaders must empower workers to take ownership of safety. This means giving workers the authority and support to make safety decisions, report hazards, and intervene when they see unsafe behavior.

- **Decentralized Safety Responsibility:** Shift some of the responsibility for safety from supervisors to individual workers. Encourage workers to actively participate in hazard identification, safety planning, and peer accountability.
- **Recognizing Safety Champions:** Acknowledge and reward workers who demonstrate a strong commitment to safety, whether through proactive hazard identification, peer interventions, or consistent adherence to protocols.

Example: A contracting company introduced a "Safety Champion" program, in which workers who went above and beyond in safety efforts were recognized at monthly meetings. This initiative encouraged workers to take personal ownership of safety and created healthy competition among teams to prioritize safety excellence.

Keeping Safety Engaging and Relevant

One of the challenges in maintaining a strong safety culture is ensuring safety remains engaging and relevant over time. Workers may become complacent, particularly after long periods without incidents, or may feel that safety procedures are repetitive or unnecessary. Keeping safety at the top of one's mind requires creative approaches to reinforce its importance.

Innovative Safety Training Programs

Traditional safety training sessions can sometimes feel monotonous, leading to disengagement. By introducing innovative and interactive methods, organizations can keep workers engaged and help them internalize safety concepts more meaningfully.

- **Hands-On Simulations:** Use realistic job simulations to allow workers to practice safety procedures in real-world settings. This reinforces knowledge and improves workers' confidence in handling safety risks.

- **Virtual Reality Training:** Emerging technologies like virtual reality (VR) can create immersive training environments where workers can practice high-risk tasks in a safe, controlled setting. VR training allows workers to experience dangerous scenarios without the actual risk.

Example: A utility company introduced virtual reality training modules where workers could practice responding to common powerline electrical hazards. Workers who completed the VR training reported feeling more confident and better prepared to manage real-life hazards, leading to a decrease in incidents.

Regular Safety Refreshers and Challenges

Regular safety refreshers, challenges, and competitions can keep safety fresh and engaging and encourage workers to think critically about safety daily.

- **Safety Competitions:** Introduce team-based safety competitions where crews compete to identify the most hazards or suggest improvements to safety procedures. Offer rewards or recognition for the teams that demonstrate the strongest safety performance.
- **Safety Days:** Host regular "Safety Days" to reinforce safety through workshops, guest speakers, and hands-on activities. These events provide a

break from the routine while keeping safety at the forefront of my mind.

Example: One company introduced an annual "Safety Challenge," where each crew submitted hazard assessments and safety improvements for review. The winning team received recognition, and their suggestions were implemented across the company, creating a sense of ownership and pride in the overall safety culture.

Embracing Technology to Enhance Safety

As technology advances, new opportunities exist to improve safety practices and sustain a strong safety culture. From wearable safety devices to real-time data analytics, integrating technology into safety management can help identify risks faster, monitor compliance, and even predict potential hazards before they occur.

Wearable Safety Technology

Wearable technology has the potential to revolutionize safety management by providing real-time data on workers' health, location, and environment. Wearables can help monitor vital signs, detect falls, and alert workers or supervisors to dangerous conditions.

- **Fall Detection Systems:** Wearable devices can automatically detect falls and send alerts to supervisors or emergency responders, ensuring a quicker response in the event of an accident.
- **Heat Stress Monitoring:** Wearables that monitor heart rate, temperature, and hydration levels can alert workers when they are at risk for heat-related illnesses, especially important in outdoor work environments.

Using Data to Predict and Prevent Incidents

Data analytics and predictive modeling are becoming increasingly important in safety management. By collecting and analyzing data from safety inspections, incident reports, and near misses, organizations can identify patterns and predict potential risks before they lead to accidents.

- **Predictive Analytics for Risk Management:** Using data to identify trends in safety incidents, such as recurring equipment failures or environmental hazards, allows companies to proactively address these risks before they result in accidents.
- **Automated Safety Alerts:** Digital safety platforms can track compliance with safety protocols in real-time, sending automated alerts when hazards are identified or when protocols are not followed.

Example: A company using predictive analytics discovered that electrical shock incidents increased when workers were under time pressure. This insight led to a revision of project timelines and additional safety training on managing stress and working safely under deadlines, reducing the overall incident rate.

Sustaining a Culture of Continuous Improvement

Sustaining a safety culture requires a mindset of **continuous improvement**. There is always room for growth; safety practices must evolve as new risks emerge. Encouraging a culture of continuous improvement means regularly evaluating safety performance, learning from past experiences, and always striving to do better.

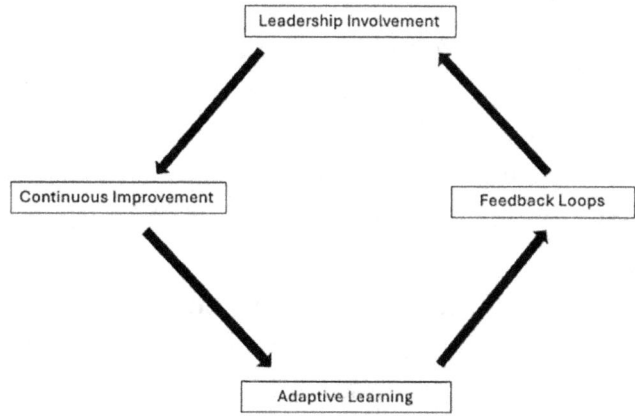

Safety Audits and Regular Assessments

Regular safety audits and assessments provide valuable insights into how well safety protocols are being followed and where improvements can be made. These audits should not be punitive but should serve as opportunities to identify weaknesses and enhance safety practices.

- **Internal and External Audits:** Conduct both internal safety audits (led by the company's safety team) and external audits (led by third-party experts) to gain an unbiased view of safety performance.
- **Using Audit Results for Improvement:** The findings from safety audits should be used to refine protocols, provide additional training, or implement new safety technologies.

Learning from Mistakes and Successes

A strong safety culture recognizes that mistakes and successes are both valuable learning tools. Organizations should celebrate safety successes while critically analyzing mistakes and near misses to extract lessons that can improve future safety performance.

- **Incident Review Processes:** After any safety incident, whether minor or major, conduct a thorough review to understand what went wrong,

why it happened, and what can be done to prevent it in the future.
- **Celebrating Successes:** Recognizing workers and teams that consistently demonstrate strong safety performance helps reinforce the idea that safety is a shared value and priority.

Example: After completing a year without a single recordable injury, one utility company held a company-wide celebration to honor the achievement. At the same time, they conducted a review of the year's near misses to ensure that lessons were learned, and potential risks were addressed before accidents could occur.

Conclusion

Sustaining a safety culture for the future is an ongoing process that requires commitment, innovation, and leadership. As the electrical utility industry evolves, so must its approach to safety. By treating safety as a dynamic process, embracing new technologies, fostering leadership engagement, and promoting continuous improvement, organizations can ensure that safety remains a core value for future generations.

Remember: safety is never "done." It is a journey that requires everyone's active participation. The steps taken today will shape the safety culture of tomorrow, ensuring that workers return home safely every single day.

References

- **OSHA Guidelines on Safety and Health Programs** (https://www.osha.gov/safety-management)
- **National Safety Council**'s resources on the importance of safety mindset and culture (https://www.nsc.org/workplace)
- **Centers for Disease Control and Prevention (CDC)** for high-risk industry safety data (https://www.cdc.gov/niosh/topics/falls/default.html)
- **Bureau of Labor Statistics (BLS)** for electrical utility industry injury statistics (https://www.bls.gov/iif/)
- **International Electrical Testing Association (NETA)** for safety standards on electrical testing (https://www.netaworld.org/standards)
- **Leadership in Safety Management** research (Hale, A. R., & Hovden, J. (1998). *Management and culture: The third age of safety. A review of approaches to organizational aspects of safety, health and environment*).
- **Transformational Leadership and Safety Behavior** (Barling, J., Loughlin, C., & Kelloway, E. K. (2002). *Development and test of a model linking safety-specific transformational leadership and occupational safety*. Journal of Applied Psychology).

References

- **Mentoring Programs in High-Risk Industries** (Ragins, B. R., & Kram, K. E. (2007). *The Handbook of Mentoring at Work: Theory, Research, and Practice*).
- **Role of Trust in Workplace Safety** (Geller, E. S. (2001). *The Psychology of Safety Handbook*).
- **The Checklist Manifesto** (Gawande, A. (2010). *The Checklist Manifesto: How to Get Things Right*).
- **National Institute for Occupational Safety and Health (NIOSH)** guides on the use of checklists (https://www.cdc.gov/niosh/).
- **National Fire Protection Association (NFPA)** reports on electrical safety incidents (https://www.nfpa.org/News-and-Research/Resources/Research-reports/Electrical)
- **Case Studies on Incident Management** from OSHA (https://www.osha.gov)
- **Continuous Improvement in Safety Management Systems** (Deming, W. E. (1986). *Out of the Crisis*).
- **National Institute of Standards and Technology (NIST)** research on evolving safety practices in high-risk industries (https://www.nist.gov).

About the Author

Bo Brown is an accomplished safety leader with over 23 years of experience in the electrical line industry. As a Certified Utility Safety Professional (CUSP), Bo is a highly respected expert in OSHA regulations and safety protocols. He is the CEO of ThinkSafe Strategies LLC, where he is dedicated to fostering a culture of safety through training, consulting, and public speaking engagements. Bo's mission is to eliminate workplace accidents in high-risk industries like electrical utilities by promoting a proactive, safety-first mindset. When not working to improve safety standards, Bo enjoys flying planes and golfing in his home state of Texas.

www.ingramcontent.com/pod-product-compliance
Lightning Source LLC
LaVergne TN
LVHW011718060526
838200LV00051B/2943